'Written with authority by a leading fi
excellent and comprehensive review of ι
sociology of childhood, and more broac
Mayall nicely locates the sociology of chi
and historical trends, thus reinforcing the ⸺ account of
childhood.'

Dr Michael Wyness, Institute of Education, University of Warwick

'With this important book, Berry Mayall has produced a timely,
comprehensive, and wide-ranging look at the emergence of the sociology
of childhood as an intellectual movement. This is a significant book for
anyone working the field of childhood studies – it establishes the intellectual
antecedents of the new sociology of childhood, links that to the field as it
stands, and then maps future directions for theoretical development. As
such, this is an important source book, but it also goes much further than
that: in setting out a thoroughly grounded history of the field it shows:
first, the significance that comes from an intellectual movement having a
historical and contemporary presence in a number of disciplinary quarters;
second, it demonstrates how the constituency of the field in current times
reflects the links between the shape of intellectual endeavour and the
politics of knowledge at any given time or place; and third, as all good
histories do, maps possible paths for the future of the area. It also grounds
the history of the sociology of childhood in wider arenas of social and
sociological concerns. A "must read" for any serious scholar engaging with
childhood studies.'

Dr Jo Moran-Ellis, University of Surrey

'This succinct account of the history of the sociology of childhood gives a
valuable and personal insight into the making of a field enquiry. It illustrates
well the contingent nature of the relationship between ideas, individuals,
and historical moments.'

Professor Allison James, University of Sheffield

'Berry Mayall's history of the sociology of childhood offers succinct and enlightening insights on the flow, movement, and interaction of ideas that have combined to form this still-growing field of scholarship. It is a resource for students and scholars alike interested in the study of children and their childhoods.'

Professor Daniel Thomas Cook, Department of Childhood Studies, Rutgers University, and co-editor of *Childhood: A Journal of Global Child Research*

A History of the Sociology of Childhood

IOEPress

A History of the Sociology of Childhood

Berry Mayall

Institute of Education Press

First published in 2013 by the Institute of Education Press,
20 Bedford Way, London WC1H 0AL
www.ioe.ac.uk/ioepress

© Berry Mayall 2013

British Library Cataloguing in Publication Data:
A catalogue record for this publication is available from the British Library

ISBNs
978-1-78277-021-3 (paperback)
978-1-78277-040-4 (PDF eBook)
978-1-78277-041-1 (ePub eBook)
978-1-78277-042-8 (Kindle eBook)

All rights reserved. No part of this publication may be reproduced, stored in a
retrieval system, or transmitted in any form or by any means, electronic, mechanical,
photocopying, recording or otherwise, without the prior permission of the
copyright owner.

Every effort has been made to trace copyright holders and to obtain their permission
for the use of copyright material. The publisher apologizes for any errors or omissions
and would be grateful if notified of any corrections that should be incorporated in
future reprints or editions of this book.

The opinions expressed in this publication are those of the authors and do not
necessarily reflect the views of the Institute of Education, University of London.

Typeset by Quadrant Infotech (India) Pvt Ltd
Printed by CPI Group (UK) Ltd, Croydon, CR0 4YY

Contents

Acknowledgements

I am very grateful to Virginia Morrow, Priscilla Alderson, and Liesbeth de Block, who each wrote paragraphs about their particular areas of expertise (see pages 17, 24 and 26 respectively). Many thanks too to Jens Qvortrup who provided me with a brief account of the development of his ideas from the 1980s onwards, which I summarize with his permission (see page 20).

About the author

Berry Mayall is Professor of Childhood Studies at the Institute of Education, University of London (IOE). She has worked for many years on research projects studying the daily lives of children and their parents. In the last 25 years she has participated in the development of the sociology of childhood, contributing many books and papers to this process, including *Towards a Sociology of Childhood* (Open University Press, 2002). *You Can Help Your Country* (IOE Press, 2011), co-authored with Virginia Morrow, is about English children's work in wartime, and is based on a sociological approach to history, and in particular explores ideas and practices about children and childhood at a time when children were not yet understood mainly as schoolchildren, but as contributors to the division of labour.

A History of the Sociology of Childhood

Introduction

This short book is written to provide some reflections on how (and to some extent why) the sociology of childhood has developed, with what precursors, and in what contexts. The rationale for writing it is that I, among others, have lived and worked through a good deal of the main period outlined here. There are many ways of approaching this topic, and in this paper I refer to some other attempts at histories. The choice of topics and works referred to is selective and relate to my own knowledge and experience. I have also consulted some scholars who, like me, have lived through the development of this field in the 1980s and onwards. So the main point of the book is to provide background information, mainly aimed at those who are engaged in studying sociological approaches to childhood.

This is a study of intellectual movements, providing some pointers to more detailed and theoretical work, which readers may wish to follow up. It contains many references, assembled to provide routes into further study. However, it does not provide complete lists; rather the idea is to point readers towards some texts that will provide them with further suggestions for reading. No doubt there is no definitive answer to the questions of how and why the sociology of childhood gathered momentum in the 1980s. Any history will vary from others. Here I suggest some enabling developments. I have focused mainly on work in English, since that is what is accessible to English speakers! And I think it is true to say that much of the work on this topic has been written in English. But the work spans not only the USA and the UK, but also work in English from the Nordic countries and from Germany. It is symptomatic of the linguistic failings of native English speakers that they do not, in general, read and take account of relevant works in other languages, notably German, and more recently French, Portuguese and Spanish. At the end of the book, I give some notes about developments in the sociology of childhood in those societies, and on research work and ideas emerging from the majority world. In a very fast-moving world, and with fast-appearing publications, I flag up in the final sections some of the important recent developments in the social worlds of childhood, notably the implications of technological inventions for the experiences of childhood, how globalization is altering the character of childhoods, and child–adult relations. These developments have been accompanied by new strands of research, including research across societies.

I note here as a disclaimer that this short book does not seek to be an introduction to 'childhood studies' or to the 'sociology of childhood'. There are many books that carry out such work. For childhood studies, we have, for instance, Mary Jane Kehily's book (2004), which complements the four course books published in connection with the Open University's BA in Childhood Studies (Woodhead and Montgomery, 2003; Maybin and Woodhead, 2003; Kehily and Swann, 2003; Montgomery, Burr and Woodhead 2003, which are currently being revised). Other key books exploring and introducing the sociology of childhood include Jenks, 1996; Corsaro, 1997 and Wyness, 2006. There is also a large literature, drawing on sociological concepts, and aimed mainly at those who work with children in various professions (for instance, Smith *et al.*, 2000; Foley, Roche, and Tucker, 2001; James and James, 2004).

It is relevant to note here at the outset why sociological approaches to childhood matter. Again, commentators will vary in their emphases, and some will put more emphasis on interesting aspects of the social construction of childhood; others will emphasize the social, economic, and political implications of children's status in societies. In my view, it is important, both socially and politically, to bring sociological thinking to childhood in order to give due recognition to children as important members of society, not as pre-social objects of socialization, but as contributing agents to the welfare of society. There are advantages to all generations and societies if we acquire greater understanding of and respect for children and for childhood (just as feminism has altered understandings of women). Children, after all, constitute about one-third of humanity, and, across the world, contribute to the economic welfare of families and societies. Most important is to recognize childhood as a permanent constitutive section of society, and to consider intergenerational relational processes between childhood and adulthood. This enterprise requires lifting children and childhood, theoretically, out of families and considering them as a social group, with their own interests, and as a social group impacted on, in ways specific to it, by macro factors: social, institutional, economic, and historic. Thus children's rights and their intersections with sociological understandings can be understood as important, indeed central, topics for investigation. In the end, the sociological study of childhood is a political enterprise, aimed at improving respect for children's rights in society, including their rights to distributive justice.

Section 1: The importance of developmental psychology in shaping childhoods

Children are of interest to adults working in a range of disciplines, and to people who work with and for children as well as to parents. The disciplines include psychology, anthropology, history, and geography as well as sociology. I shall include some notes on these disciplines later, but any survey of this kind has to start with some general points about developmental psychology.

It has been suggested that social groups in society become of interest to academics/researchers/sociologists/politicians when they present a problem, or where social and economic changes alter relations between social groups (Zinnecker, 1990; Wyness, 2006). Children became of intense interest in the last quarter of the nineteenth century in minority world societies, we may argue, because the whole population of children became exposed to the adult gaze when universalist education services were developed. This was also the case in England, because the demands of industry and empire led to growing state concern about the moral, mental, and physical health of the nation (Hendrick, 1994, chapter 2). However, as Erica Burman (1994: 10–12) describes, earlier in the nineteenth century, scholars had begun to concern themselves with the study of infants, as part of a current interest in considering the relative importance of genetic endowment and environmental experience. Darwin studied one of his children and provided the first published diary of infancy in 1877 (a compilation of notes made in 1840). Propositions within the child-study movement included the idea that very young children, having had little time to learn, were close to nature and so provided a route into adult understanding of what it is to be human. More specifically, studies of young children aimed to discover 'the origins and specificities of mind, that is, the adult mind' (Burman, 1994: 10). Furthermore, the child-study movement, one of the bases of the discipline of developmental psychology, explored a concept of development – both individual and evolutionary – that was characterized by ordered, directed steps up a hierarchy. Indeed Morss (1990: chapter 2) has argued that the effect of Darwin's work was to reinforce a version of biology that emphasized similarity in progression towards adulthood, rather than variation. Child-study societies began to observe, weigh, and measure children – procedures that became more feasible as all children became sited in educational institutions. And, as Burman comments (1994: 11), this movement reflected an understanding of and reliance on a particular idea about 'science', as a set of practices associated with the modern state.

Histories of developmental psychology abound. Erica Burman's (1994: chapter 1; second edition, 2007) is a good, constructively critical one, and she also provides a concise, useful further reading list. Her history covers the rise of the child-study movement in the mid- to late-nineteenth century; the dominance of men, who provided a 'scientific', detached gaze; how psychology developed to meet social concerns; the rise of testing linked to the notion of the normal child; the growing interest in how children move from infancy to adulthood; and the naturalization and normalization of childhood through the provision and practices of kindergartens. Another account covering this ground is given by Alan Prout (2005: chapter 2). See also the early chapters of Harry Hendrick's *Child Welfare* (2003). Martin Woodhead, who has played a central part in constructing the Open University multidisciplinary degree course on Childhood, has provided useful discussions of child development, tracing crucial elements in its history and its interrelations with childhood studies (e.g. Woodhead, 2003).

Woodhead (2009) identifies three major priorities in child development research from the early twentieth century. The first was to describe the main developmental 'milestones', and this was done using observational methods, with Arnold Gesell as a pioneer in the early twentieth century. The second priority was to explain these patterns of development, to consider theories that would account for them. At one extreme were maturationist theories that rested on the idea of a genetically encoded development plan, while at the other were environmentalist theories, emphasizing the influences of learning and experience. A third priority has been to measure the impact of environmental factors in shaping individual differences.

In providing some kinds of knowledge about children, psychology is the dominant discipline and is linked to service provision. That is, those who work with and for children (for instance in health, education, and welfare) tend to be trained within psychological paradigms, and other services that deal with children, such as legal services and the police, call on psychologists as expert witnesses. This linkage of theory, or discipline, with practice both underscores psychology's legitimacy and has given it great power to control knowledge and affect people's lives. For most people in minority world societies (western European countries and North America), developmental psychology provides the basis of their understanding of children and of childhood. It can be argued that politicians and other policy-makers too rely on psychological ideas, and that these influence the policies and practices they put in place. Thus, for instance, children in schools are sorted into age groups, in line with the idea that their stage of development will be common to them and some whose stage of development is regarded as abnormal may be given help to achieve normality.

A further general point is that psychological approaches to children and childhood were worked up mainly in minority world societies. What has often been presented as fact can also be read as stories based on assumptions and practices. Thus, for instance, emphasis on children's 'need' for maternal care reflects societies where the individual mother sited in a nuclear family is generally allocated the responsibility for the care of her children; in some societies, a wider range of women take responsibility for childcare, and beliefs and practices reflect this (e.g. Gottlieb, 2004). A useful book on this topic is Bradley's (1989) *Visions of Infancy,* which analyses ideas about childcare across time in minority world societies, pointing out that they can be seen less as facts and more as stories that fit their times and places. It has also been argued that the UN Convention on the Rights of the Child (UNCRC) is based unduly on minority world psychological ideas (Stephens, 1995), for instance in playing down children's responsibilities and, again, assuming the nuclear family as a desirable norm. However, this argument has been discussed and modified in more recent analyses of children's rights across the world (e.g. Liebel, 2012). As noted above, at the end of the book I include some reflections on globalization and on sociological and rights-related work emerging from the majority world, and how this is relevant material for modifying minority world approaches and understandings.

Section 2: Precursors of sociological approaches to childhood – especially in the USA

Histories of developing interest in sociological approaches to childhood will vary in their focus, and will be influenced by the author's knowledge and interests. The Swiss researcher Cléopatre Montandon (1998) – who has lived and worked in the USA – provides a useful paper on the importance of English-language work and especially of US scholars as precursors of the sociology of childhood. She refers to a paper on early twentieth century interest in childhood as a social phenomenon by Trent (1987) – who locates that interest in the work of US scholars in the 1920s and 1930s. Against the background of the dominance of developmental psychology, he says that these scholars argued for sociological approaches, but that this interest then declined, which can be ascribed to several causes. Psychology, already well established as an academic discipline, also had bases in professional work with children – hence great power and prestige. Psychologists were thereby able to commandeer financial resources for further academic and policy-related work – to the detriment of sociologists. He also argues that methodologically, sociological work (with its suggestions and theoretical frameworks) was socially less acceptable than the positivist, hard-fact-finding work of psychology. He also sees as relevant the decline of the 1920s Chicago school of sociology, to which these men belonged and which focused on symbolic interactionism; and the rise of functionalism (Parsons) (for instance see Craib, 1992: chapter 5 for discussion). Functionalism proposed a clear pre-social position and status for children, under the power of adults – an appealing theory for adults keen to maintain power. The strong hold (at any rate in the USA) of the notion that socialization consists of transmission from adult to child – the child as empty vessel – is demonstrated in a thorough review of the literature by Clausen (1968). April Brayfield (1998), who analysed key words in papers in the US *Journal of Marriage and the Family*, found almost no mention of children as other than socialization projects, over nearly 60 years of the journal's issues to 1997. She attributed this absence of recognition of children as social agents to the structural functionalist leanings of successive editors of the journal. We may note in passing that the factors Trent identified, in maintaining the dominance of psychological approaches to childhood in the USA, still look relevant today, for that country has been slow to respond to the sociological work done in Europe during the last 25 years (Bass, 2010). However (no doubt among other initiatives), three academic centres in the USA stand out for their pioneering work. A department of child studies with an interdisciplinary approach has been established at Rutgers University in New Jersey; Bill Corsaro has established childhood study courses at Indiana University; and Barrie Thorne and colleagues have carried out important research work on children as migrants at the University of California, Berkeley and Los Angeles (e.g. Orellana, 2011).

Although there are other disciplines with an interest in childhood (see below), it is not surprising that it is the characteristics of traditional developmental psychology that have frequently been the target of critical comment, since they have had great, and some would say, detrimental influences, as well as positive influences. Clearly, positive influences include recognition of children as engaged in learning, in travelling along pathways towards adulthood; also beneficial is that children are not to be judged according to criteria applying to adults. For instance, up to certain ages (which vary across societies), children are not judged by adults as competent to accept criminal responsibility. And the points made by Eglantyne Jebb in her 1924 Declaration of the Rights of the Child still hold: adults have a responsibility to protect children and to provide for them, since children's biological vulnerability demands this response. Essentially, perhaps, the adverse criticisms focus on the point that, in its traditional manifestations, developmental psychology was too certain that it was describing universals; it was partial in its focus; and it did not fit with people's observations of children in their daily lives and activities (e.g. Morss, 1990, 1996; Greene, 1999). It provided justifications for adult dominance over children, for denying them personhood, and for the institutionalization of childhood. It emphasized children's deficits by contrast with adults' competencies. It focused on problems and interventions devised to address these and to bring children back to normality (for discussion see for instance Prout and James, 1997; Hutchby and Moran-Ellis, 1998). Arlene Skolnick (1975), a US research psychologist, wrote an important paper on how children's lives had become separated from those of adults, resulting, in her view, from the consolidation of developmental perspectives. Her paper details how psychological theorists in the late nineteenth and early twentieth centuries argued that children differed fundamentally from adults, as incompetent and dependent creatures; and many eminent psychologists argued that children's development was intrinsically linked to biologically rooted functions, which organized and controlled development. Much of the work was laboratory-based and context-free. And much of it owed a lot to evolutionary theory, which saw in the development of individual children, the development of mankind. As Kessen put it (1965: 115):

> From the publication of *The Origin of Species* (Darwin) to the end of the nineteenth century, there was a riot of parallel-drawing between animal and child, between primitive man and child, between early human history and child. The developing human being was seen as a natural museum of human phylogeny and history; by careful observation of the infant and child, one could see the descent of man.

A detailed account of this proposition is given by Morss (1990). Another important paper on this history is by Anne-Marie Ambert (1986), a Canadian scholar, who documented the 'near absence' of studies on children in mainstream sociology by studying classical sociologists' work, introductory textbooks, and journals (mainly from the USA). (This absence is still to be seen in some UK textbooks, though journals are catching up.) Again, like Brayfield, she found little apart from work within 'socialization', which, as she says, is not about childhood but about how people become adults. She notes male dominance in sociology, the high status of macro-sociology and career issues: 'One does not become a household name in sociology by studying children' (24). She notes that although one might expect feminism to be interested in children, in fact it has focused on adults and gender roles;

women 'had to labor within the constraints of a pre-existing, patriarchal gate-keeping system' (24). Ambert's was a forward-looking paper, but it is limited in that her only suggestion for sociology to engage with children was for studies of children's own worlds and of children's views of their social worlds – we may refer here to the work of Iona and Peter Opie (e.g. 1969) and to the 'tribal' worlds approach described by James, Jenks, and Prout (1998: 28). The leap towards the study of children and childhood as part of the social structure had yet to be taken.

During the 1960s and 1970s, however,[1] as Skolnick (1975) describes, a number of observers, from a range of disciplines, continued to critique the dominant psychological positions. Allport (1968), for instance, said that findings within psychology were not facts, but rather ideas that drew on social and political contexts. Hillary Rodham – now Clinton – noted in 1970 that the ideology of dependency fostered by developmentalism provided a justification for denying children their rights. David J. Rothman (1971) argued that age-grading children and siting them in age-related institutions constitutes one form of adult social control over children, rather than a natural response to the laws of development. A major critique of standard developmental psychology – as carried out in the USA up until the 1970s at least – was that it was mainly laboratory-based, and that researchers adopted a partial approach – that is, they focused only on specific aspects of children's lives and activities. Thus Jean Piaget focused on cognitive development, others on attachment behaviour, but in general psychologists were not concerned with the whole child and her everyday activities in everyday contexts. A striking catchphrase was developed by von Bertalanffy (1960): the 'nothing but' fallacy. This means that the bits and pieces of children's lives studied by psychologists were seen to constitute the whole child. Thus, for instance, while the 'scientist' might focus on eating and sleep in a newborn's life, other observers, working from differing perspectives or with differing aims, found evidence of playful activity early on: so it could be argued that children's lives were more complex than a focus on one or two features might suggest (Skolnick, 1975: 53–5) and included, as well as the physical, a child's active engagement with the world.

A further major critique of developmental psychology as practised in the USA up to the 1970s was that it was a-historic. That is, it failed to be aware of its own intellectual and ideological commitments and assumptions. This point was made in a number of books and papers reflecting on the discipline's history (e.g. Sampson, 1981; Kessel and Siegel, 1983; Bronfenbrenner *et al.*,

---

[1] This paragraph draws on Skolnick's (1975) account and on her references.

1986). Very interesting are papers given at a 1987 conference in which US historians and psychologists discussed their disciplines and what possibilities they could identify for collaboration; at the end of the conference, Michael Zuckerman reflected on the papers and noted that historians could perhaps help psychologists, by stressing 'what many historians take for granted and indeed know in their bones: that human behaviour is invincibly contingent and that social action is crucially conditioned by context' (Zuckerman, 1993: 231).

In the 1970s developmental psychology began to move out of the laboratory and into everyday life, perhaps partly under the influence of these critiques; possibly also because children in day-care institutions were increasingly available for study. Perhaps, too, as more women entered research work, bringing their own experiences of living with children, they could see advantages in studying children in their natural environments. Work on socialization had previously relied heavily on mothers' accounts, and it began to be clear that observation in ordinary contexts might redress bias in these accounts (Danziger, 1970: 25). A key point is that critics had challenged the 'isolability' of 'the' child and had urged that social context was more than 'context' or background, but also constituted a focus for children's interactions and learning (Bronfenbrenner, 1979; see Greene, 1999 for a history of these developments; also more recently Greene, 2006). This new focus on children as interactive social beings in their everyday lives and learning began to enter works on 'socialization', which was now becoming understood centrally as a two-way process. Danziger (1971: 61–2) noted children's power from birth to influence events as social actors – through their cries and smiles: 'Parent and child form a system in which both partners control and socialize each other and both are dispensers of rewards and sources of information.' (See also papers in Danziger's [1970] edited collection; here the paper by Chombard de Lauwe focuses on children's activity in socialization processes.) Denzin (1977) observed and interacted with his own young children and made a powerful case for the agency of children, especially their activity in developing social relations. Elkin and Handel (1978; first published 1960) noted that it is through children's human ability to act as social beings in interaction with others that learning – of social norms, morality, the social world – takes place. An interesting PhD (Flapan, 1968), again within broadly developmental psychological approaches, shows children's ability to describe and analyse social encounters (she showed children film clips and asked them – aged 6, 9, and 12 – to comment) and how the subtlety of these accounts increases the older the children are. Judging by the rows of books in university libraries on socialization, many of which identify children's agency in the socialization process, it was a very short step not taken to theorize children as agents in social worlds, and to study them more broadly in the course of their peer interactions and child–adult interactions, and in the constructions of their lives in those worlds.

An important scholar who challenged psychological assumptions is Michael Cole; he carried out studies from the 1960s onwards in a range of cultures. His arguments and evidence are complex, and I recommend Sheldon White's Foreword to Cole's 1996 book for clarification, as well as Cole's own chapter 1. As Cole says, he built on the concepts of the Russian psychologist Vygotsky, whose work he knew well – he translated much of it for western readers. Vygotsky argued from the 1920s onwards that students of people must understand human mental life as deeply connected to the objects of human manufacture in the world around us. Traditional psychology had been 'naturalistic', rooted in biological processes and developments: it studied sensations, associations, reflexes, or sensorimotor schemes. But, Cole argues, we also need a second kind of psychology, which considers how mental processes are formed by culture (and are therefore not universal). This point resonates with Michael Zuckerman's comment quoted above.

One of the ways in which psychological assumptions were opened up for reconsideration in the post-Second World War years was through the study of children's lives in varying societies. An important interest among American psychologists was in a range of child-rearing/socialization aims and methods in differing countries (see Mead and Wolfenstein, 1955; Whiting, 1963). Why did this interest develop? Perhaps one cause was that Americans (like everyone else) perceived that there were social problems in their country, especially those involving young people (problematizing and blaming children is not [entirely] confined to the UK), and wondered how other societies fared and coped. Some psychologists had come to the USA from other societies; it seems they maintained an interest in the world beyond the USA and had the linguistic competence to study it. Bruno Bettelheim, a concentration camp survivor, was a dedicated academic working for children in the United States, and thought 'slum children' posed a serious problem in that country. He (together with colleagues) identified the Israeli kibbutz as a natural experiment in child-rearing, and he sought to consider whether communal child-rearing challenged the American model of the family and its (possibly detrimental) power over children. His work on this topic began in the 1950s and led to *The Children of the Dream*, first published in the UK in 1969. He identifies the separation (in the USA) of child cohorts from adult cohorts as a principal source of social problems – notably disaffected children. He refers to Ariès (1962; also published in English in the US in 1962), who described the common activities and common interests of children and adults in pre-industrial (French) society. He suggests that the solidarity of interest between people of all ages (as exemplified in the kibbutz, where everyone works for the common good) is a key to the healthy development of children (1969: 58 *et seq.*). This idea has important resonance for today's minority world societies: that we would do well to revive practices and policies based on people's contributions to the division of labour, including the contributions of children, working alongside adults. As others have noted, giving children serious things to do in society constitutes an important way of including children in socially valued activity, as well as respecting their participation rights (Holdsworth, 2005).

Urie Bronfenbrenner, another US psychologist, was born in Russia, emigrated aged 6 with his family to the US, and grew up in a house attached to an institution for the 'feeble minded', where his father was a neuropathologist. He visited Russia to study their nurseries, which operated on the communist ideal of rearing children to be good Soviet citizens, and he made a comparison between the USSR and the USA in respect of their child-rearing ideas and practices (Bronfenbrenner, 1971).There was also a psychological expedition to China to study group-rearing of children there (Kessen, 1975).

During this period, there was also academic interest in how childhood has been presented in philosophical works across the ages – again, these are minority-world works – where children are seen mainly as socialization projects (Kessen, 1965; Jenks, 1982). Kessen's book is firmly sited within child psychology in the minority world, and he quotes from key figures in its history, noting the wide range of influences on its development (medicine, philosophy, pedagogy, child study, the measurement of children, psychoanalysis) (1965: ix). Jenks (1982) also quotes pronouncements on childhood across the European ages and offers an insightful overview. What both these books also do is more generally draw attention to variation in ideas and practices in child-rearing and child–adult relations. In other words, they introduce social constructionism into ideas about childhood. Chris Jenks told me once that upon publication in 1982, his book 'fell like a stone'; its time had not yet come. It was re-issued in the early 1990s: perhaps its time had then come, for by this time childhood had begun to take its place in sociology, though still as a very minor component. Jenks' own exploration of the social construction of childhood (Jenks, 1996) used some of the earlier material he had collated, together with an investigation of the implications of the murder in 1993 of James Bulger by two boys (aged 10), for public understandings in the UK about children and childhood.

Of course, meanwhile, anthropologists had been drawing attention to differing child experiences in other than minority world societies. Thus Margaret Mead's book on Samoan society (first published in 1928) argued that the problematic stage of 'adolescence' (as propagated in the USA, notably by G. Stanley Hall [1904], but perhaps first described by Rousseau) did not exist in Samoa. Anthropologists studying many societies described the transition from the status of 'child' to 'adult' as taking place at the time of puberty, with no intervening 'adolescent' stage; and children's engagement with the social and economic work of their household and society was a means whereby they (as in Ariès' pre-industrialized France) participated as soon as they physically could, rather than being sited in a pre-social sphere. Critiques of the concept of adolescence abound (e.g. Musgrove, 1964; Keniston, 1971), and an important basis for their critique is the study of other societies where:

> The social sphere of adult and child is unitary and undivided ... Nothing in the universe of adult behaviour is hidden from children or barred to them. They are actively and responsibly part of the social structure, the economic system, the ritual and ideological system (Fortes, 1970).

This work may be seen within the context of developments in sociological theory, which challenged the structural functionalist approach to how society works, as proposed by Parsons (1951). His ontological analysis suggests a coherent, constructive set of social institutions that cement people into their adult roles as conforming members of society. He presents the family (and later the school) as key institutions, since they socialize children to take their place as functioning and conforming members of society. In the 1960s, scholars began to question this vision. The social interactionist tradition, started in the Chicago school of sociology in the 1920s, was revived in the 1960s. The central, epistemological idea was that people act on the basis of the meanings they find in social life; these meanings are constructed through human interaction. Goffman made an influential examination of how social constructionism works. He studied how institutions successfully turn people into inmates who learn to operate within the rules (overt and covert) of the institution; thus he consolidated the concept of institutionalization (*Asylums*, 1961) and explored how within human encounters, we structure our own identities and those of other people (*Encounters*, 1961). The power of interactional processes between people to form their identities was elaborated and exemplified in labelling theory, where people's social status is achieved through the actions of others in identifying them as a certain kind of person (Becker, 1963; 1967) – a person who is socially understood or described as 'bad' is one who has successfully been labelled (identified) as bad. The career of someone as a drug-taker or criminal is that of one who has continually been identified as that sort of person and whose membership of that group is reinforced by labelling processes. (For a more recent summary of work on social identity, see, for instance, Jenkins, 1996.) These ideas provided a platform for considering children as interactive people; and indeed the negotiations that people engage in to confirm and to challenge their social status is an important theme in Bourdieu's work, referred to later.

Section 3: Sociological approaches to childhood in the UK – early days

I would suggest that by the 1970s and 1980s, there was considerable support for the idea that children should be conceptualized as active agents in learning, through interactions with family and friends. An important UK researcher was Barbara Tizard (1984) who, with Martin Hughes, investigated how four-year-olds learn, by studying their conversations with their teachers at nursery and with their mothers at home. They found that much more complex conversations took place at home than at nursery, and they attributed this to the strength of mother–child relations and to the fact that children and their mothers share experiences in the events of daily life. Another pioneer is Judy Dunn (1988, 2004) who studied the social worlds and experiences of babies and toddlers, with a particular focus on children's moral learning in interaction with their siblings and mothers. As noted above, social constructionism had drawn attention to variations in concepts of childhood. Now these two strands – social constructionism and children as agents – became two of the building blocks of the sociology of childhood; the third is a structural approach – and its time had not yet come. So epistemology, the study of our experiential and theoretical knowledge, predominated over ontology, which is the study of which social forces structure our lives and how they do so.

In the UK in the 1970s and 1980s, social interactionism and Michel Foucault were influential. And one branch of sociology began to take an interest in children as more than objects of adult socialization activities: medical sociology. Here scholars were investigating what was going on in people's encounters with health or education professionals, using interactionism and social constructionism, and studying power relations in these encounters.

Medical sociology – or the sociology of health and healing

Medical sociology has been for many years the biggest branch of sociology in the UK. It has included work on how people are positioned in their encounters with doctors, and especially with power relations in these encounters. A group of scholars (Armstrong, Strong and Silverman) carried out detailed observational studies of these encounters, including some in child-health clinics. Although their principal interest was in the adults involved (mothers and doctors, mainly), they began to observe how the child was positioned and even constructed (Strong, 1979; Silverman, 1987). Armstrong wrote an important book (1983) on the social construction of people in clinics, including a chapter on children that analysed the historical development of child surveillance (including testing) and its impact on how children were understood. A pioneering paper by May and Strong (1980) described some characteristics of how we as adults view children, and the historical origins of these views; they analysed the power interests shaping our views; and noted how childhood is defined by these views. In my own work I built on these studies (e.g. Mayall, 1998).

A critical contribution within medical sociology was made by the feminist sociologist Margaret Stacey. She reconsidered the division of labour to include women (whose work in the domestic, or private, domain was devalued in mainstream sociology), and briefly alluded to the desirability of including children too in the division of labour (1980: 187). Her work on the division of labour in the health-care field challenged the identification of people as 'patients' (suffering objects of professional care) and redefined them as active in their own health care (maintenance, promotion, and repair). Women should be defined as health carers in daily life in the home, and as carers both for and about other household members (she called this 'people work'). This argument is given detailed treatment by Hilary Graham (1984). Stacey's feminist work on allied topics is collected in her textbook *The Sociology of Health and Healing* (1988), where, in the light of her early empirical work in children's hospitals, she briefly discusses child–adult relations at home in contrast to those in hospital, notes that children have some opportunities for agency at home, and considers children's agency in trying to improve child–adult relations in hospital (204–5).

Feminism and childhood – a difficult relationship between disciplines

The feminist movement that began in the USA in the late 1960s and became important in Europe in the early 1970s was concerned above all with the social and political status of women, and used as its principal analytic tool the idea of gender as distinct from sex, where sex refers to physical difference and gender refers to the socially constructed differences between men and women, organized in favour of the power of men. One of its key contributions was the theory, notably propounded by Dorothy Smith, that to understand the social position and experience of a minority social group, one has to listen to their accounts and to work these up, using study of the structures of society, into an analysis of the standpoint (including viewpoint) of this group. (See Smith, 1988, and my summary notes in my 2002 book: chapter 7.) In working with women in everyday contexts, and analysing everyday life as problematic (Smith, 1988), researchers provided detailed accounts of mothers' lives with their children, and these also threw light on how mothers themselves understand their children – as people, rather than projects, as contributors to social relations, and as competent members of the household (Boulton, 1983; Mayall and Foster, 1989; Halldén, 1991; Ribbens, 1994). Indeed it can be argued that children, like women, carry out 'people work' in caring for household members and in caring about them (Mayall, 2002: chapter 5).

However, it has remained the case that feminists have been wary of working *for* children (for discussion see Thorne and Contratto, 1982; Alanen, 1992, 1994). One central concern for feminists has been to challenge the assumption that women are the natural caretakers of young children (they have insisted on separating the biological from the social). But to the extent to which feminists took account of the common (minority world) assumption that children 'need' mothers, they had to define children as adversaries (see for discussion Alanen, 1992: 32 and Mayall, 2002: 167 *et seq.*). However, it does seem to me important that feminists take part in reconceptualizing children and childhood in relational terms, since women's relations with children are an important – even central – part of the common experiences of women, and these relations continue to be important – even central – across the life course.

In spite of this wariness, it has been argued (Therborn, 1993, 1996) that whilst feminism did not aim to fight battles directly for children, nevertheless it has opened up the family for inspection by problematizing it. For in challenging the patriarchal organization of the family as it affected women, feminists also raised questions about the status of children within the family: what were the characteristics of child–adult relations in the family? And what were children's experiences of life within the family? Further, in the wake of the massive development of childcare centres in European societies from the 1970s onwards, women can be seen as key players in posing questions about what kinds of childhoods societies were providing, and whether they were good childhoods. If children were to spend large parts of the day in childcare centres, then this raised urgent questions for women, men, and also government: How should responsibility for the rearing of children be divided between parents, the state, and private/voluntary agencies, and what constituted good child-rearing – in all settings? These questions have largely been, if not solved, then muted in many European countries, where children's attendance at childcare centres is accepted as normal, though in the UK, where governments have been slow to provide childcare centres, debates continue. And of course, a huge amount of social science research has taken place as the generality of preschool children became readily visible and accessible to researchers. Such research has commonly focused on children as social agents, on children's friendships, and on child–adult relations (from the massive literature, here are a few examples, mainly with a cross-national slant and comprising political commentary, all of which will lead the reader on to other studies: New and David, 1985; Penn, 2000; Cohen *et al.*, 2004; Yelland, 2010).

Historical studies

We should also note the importance of historians in opening up varieties of childhood for inspection. Again much of this work is about minority world societies. Since Ariès' *Centuries of Childhood* was published in English in 1962, it has been a key point of reference for anyone interested in how childhood has changed over the centuries. His analysis (focusing on France) is complex, but essentially he argued that our 'modern' ways of understanding childhood – as a distinct period of life with its own institutions and practices – developed over several centuries, perhaps starting in the fourteenth century. Before that, children joined in with the work and amusements of people generally, as soon as they physically could. The development of schools and of the idea of the family (in the sixteenth and seventeenth centuries), and of concepts associated with these, helped to separate out childhood from adulthood.

An important contribution to this historical work was made by the economist Viviana Zelizer (1985), who studied how children in the cities of the USA were removed from active contributions to working and public life at the start of the twentieth century, and were relegated to childhood at school and at home. This work, in the Ariès tradition, discusses the changing valuation of children, from economic contributors to society to 'priceless' assets for parents who are highly prized within the family. She has since revisited the field in her discussion of the economic status and contributions of children nowadays in the United States (2005).

Historian Harry Hendrick (1990/97) has provided clear accounts of changes in models of childhood in England over two centuries (see also Cunningham, 1991) and has traced these models during successive recent

Conservative and Labour governments (Hendrick, 2003). Anna Davin (1990) gives a fascinating account of how working-class and middle-class children, and especially girls, were differently conceptualized in late nineteenth century England, and how their lives differed.

The ethnography of childhood

It is relevant to note here the initiatives and influence of anthropologists in moving the study of childhood onwards. Thus Jean La Fontaine, anthropologist at the London School of Economics, organized meetings in the 1980s to discuss new ideas about childhood, and she wrote a chapter for an important book of papers on childhoods in social contexts (La Fontaine, 1986). She was perhaps one of the first to emphasize that the notion of 'child' is relational; it refers to the relational role of child – vis-à-vis adults or parents (1986: 20). A later paper used anthropological theory on personhood to consider how far children have been and can be considered to hold the status of a person, given that they are not ascribed socially valued activities in some societies (La Fontaine, 1999).

In England[2] another key development was a series of workshops organized by Judith Ennew, the first in Cambridge (1986). These were meetings of professionals and academics. Ennew is a social anthropologist who had undertaken studies relating to child workers, 'street children', and child sexual exploitation, and she was concerned about the poor knowledge-base – both theoretical and methodological – about children and childhood. The purpose of the first meeting was to discuss appropriate methods for studying the differing social and cultural influences on the institution of childhood. The participants, who came from voluntary and statutory services as well as from the international community and academic institutions, were aiming to provide a social perspective on childhood – using children as the units of analysis and statistics – which would complement the existing medical, psychological, and educational models. A second workshop was held in 1987 in Canada, a third in Cambridge in 1988, a fourth in Zimbabwe in 1989, and much later the fifth, Asia-Pacific Childhoods, was held in Singapore in 2006.

These first meetings gathered together some of the people who then worked on Jens Qvortrup's Childhood as a Social Phenomenon programme (see below) and wrote the country reports; for instance Judith Ennew (England and Wales), Giovanni Sgritta and Angelo Saporiti (Italy), Anne Solberg (Norway), David Oldman (Scotland), and Marjatta Bardy (Finland). The workshops also provided material and contributors for the edited collection of papers by Allison James and Alan Prout (both anthropologists

---

[2] Virginia Morrow has contributed the next two paragraphs.

by training), which was first published in 1990. Thus at the 1988 workshop the following contributors to that book were present: Allison James and Alan Prout, Jo Boyden, Harry Hendrick, Anne Solberg, Benno Glauser and Jens Qvortrup.

We may also note that another key meeting that brought together people interested in new ideas about childhood was the final meeting to discuss the approaches and findings of the Childhood as a Social Phenomenon programme (1992, Billund, Denmark). Some of these people, for instance Allison James, Alan Prout, and Chris Jenks, later collaborated (1998). (See below for paragraphs about Jens Qvortrup.)

It is perhaps relevant to note, through a personal anecdote, that the ideas propagated through these varying ventures were readily accessible by the early 1980s to anyone interested in pursuing them. In 1980 I was writing up my PhD, which drew on an empirical study (with Pat Petrie) on mothers' and childminders' ideas about children and childcare. This study revealed marked differences between the two groups, and led me to consider social constructions of childhood and devote one chapter of the PhD to the history of ideas about childhood (see also Mayall and Petrie, 1983). Contacts with a range of academics encouraged me, ten years later in 1990, to start a seminar series on childhood and later on, Alan Prout and I continued to run the series with ESRC funding. These meetings, over four to five years, probably also helped to develop ideas and certainly allowed people to get together and discuss their work. For an overview of sociological work on childhood in the UK, see Jo Moran-Ellis' 2010 paper in *Current Sociology*.

Section 4: Childhood sociology in (other) north European countries

By the 1980s, it appears that information and ideas were coming in from many sides (see for instance Richards, 1974; Richards and Light, 1986). Psychology itself was becoming more aware of children as social actors. Anthropology and history showed that childhoods differ at differing times and places. Histories of medicine showed how adult concerns shaped childhoods and how the establishment of institutions in line with those concerns exerted powerful influences on ideas about childhood. Thus scholars in the 1980s had a sound basis for ideas about children as agents, and about childhood as a social construction.

If we take up again the earlier suggestion (see section 1) that it is often as a social problem that a social group captures the attention of scholars, then we could say that by the 1980s, childhood was perceived to have reached a new crisis as western countries increasingly scholarized and institutionalized children's childhoods. In the Nordic countries, an international study – the BASUN project – considered what their societies were doing to childhood, in the wake of the rapid expansion of childcare centres (Dencik, 1989); and the Swedish sociologist Rita Liljeström (1983) mounted an attack on the institutionalization of children in Swedish childcare centres. The particular and peculiar English slant on these issues (under a Conservative government) consisted of worry about maternal deprivation and the decline of family values. Germany had not yet embarked on massive institutionalization of young children, but had its own concerns (see below). France had long had universalist childcare centres, including the *écoles maternelles,* but had not yet embarked on sociological research on early childhood (for consideration of scholarization in French *écoles maternelles* since the 1970s, see Garnier, 2011).

At any rate, the great move forward was to reconsider childhood as part of the social structure of society. As noted above, feminists had briefly alluded to this topic but had not developed it fully. Probably, these structural approaches were first most fully developed in Germany, and notably their work included the study of intersections of the structural with the experiential. In the 1970s, a group of sociologists began to consider why it was that concepts of childhood and how people lived their childhoods had changed during their lifetime (for an account of the study, see Zeiher, 2003). They studied two generations of children: those born before or just around the start of the Second World War (as they themselves were), and that generation's children born in the 1960s. Germany had had a momentous, dramatic history, with fascism and the war in the 1930s and 1940s, then a post-war attempt by men to reimpose patriarchy in families, and then a huge move in the 1960s towards democratization. These sociologists sought to consider how the character and experiences of childhood in the two periods related to the larger structures within which childhoods were lived (Preuss-Lausitz *et al.,* 1983). They saw, in the tradition of Mannheim, that generations of people responded to social and political movements and formed new kinds of generations (Zeiher, 2003, 2010). The German sociologists were perhaps the first to carry out systematic research that related empirical work on the daily lives and perspectives of children to the social structures with which children's lives and agency interacted (see for descriptions and discussion Zeiher, 2010). However, until the late 1990s, most of this work was published only in German, and in the UK it was virtually unknown till then.

I flag up here the theme of generation in European work. The work in Germany drew attention to interlinked levels of generational relations at the personal and family level as well as the structural level. This work has been continued over the years (see papers in Qvortrup *et al.,* 1994; Mayall and

Zeiher, 2003; Qvortrup *et al.*, 2009). Work on generation allows us to consider interconnections and interdependencies. An important scholar here is the Finnish sociologist Leena Alanen. She has consistently argued for relational sociologies, and in particular for intergenerational relational studies, firmly based on a structural approach to societal workings (Alanen, 2003, 2009, 2011). This work has been complemented by studies of intergenerational redistributive justice, with particular emphasis on how, in 'ageing' welfare states, the elderly receive more from the national wealth than children do (Qvortrup, 1994; Sgritta, 1994; Olk, 2009).

In work published in English, a key pioneer is the Danish sociologist Jens Qvortrup. He has provided me with a brief account of the development of his ideas from the 1980s, which I summarize here with his permission. Qvortrup's sociological work had been grounded in Marxism, and he had worked on social structure and welfare in socialist countries. In the 1980s, he went to the European Centre in Vienna to direct two projects: on divorce and changing family patterns. He was amazed to find that scholars working on 'the family' were interested in children only as problems for parents (costs, barriers to careers, childcare issues). This led him to begin to formulate ideas about how to include children within sociology, and he published a first paper on his ideas about a sociology of childhood in 1985 – in English. During his years in Vienna, Qvortrup worked with Helmut Wintersberger and Giovanni Sgritta, who shared his interest in a macro approach to childhood. Wintersberger was influential in securing some financial funding at the European Centre in Vienna for the five-year macro-level project, Childhood as a Social Phenomenon (CSP), which ran from 1987–92 and included 16 western industrialized countries. Scholars from each country investigated five main topics: the sociography of childhood, the activities of childhood, distributive justice, the economics of childhood, and the legal status of childhood. Each country produced a report, and further publications emerged from related conferences (Qvortrup, 1993; Wintersberger, 1996). *Childhood Matters* (Qvortrup *et al.*, 1994) provided papers by participants in the CSP on themes arising from the work. Both Sgritta and Wintersberger wrote a number of papers on the macro-analysis of childhood (see Qvortrup, 1994; Sgritta, 1994; Wintersberger, 1996). This work has been very important in its focus on childhood as a social status, the economics of childhood, intergenerational justice, and children as a generational group. It provided an approach and knowledge of more general import than empirical studies of children as social agents, or on children and childhoods as social constructions, and it provided a firm basis for the consideration of childhood as minority status within social structures and relations.

It is relevant to add here some notes on Qvortrup's 1985 paper. He used a macro-historical analysis of children as workers in order to reconsider children's contributions to the division of labour in present-day industrialized societies. Children who, over the centuries, had contributed to household and national economies through their work in households, fields, and factories, now contributed through their agency as workers at school, acquiring the necessary knowledge for their future lives as workers. This idea challenged the notion that schooling is socialization (as proposed by Durkheim, 1961) and that the main workers in schools are the teachers (see also Oldman, 1994). The understanding of children as contributors to the division of labour has been a central topic in the sociology of childhood, and it has been found that whilst scholarization continues apace, and more of the world's children attend schools, most children across the world do some kind of other work, whether paid or unpaid, during their childhood (e.g. Morrow, 1994, 1996; Mizen *et al.*, 2001; Lavalette *et al.*, 1995; Woodhead, 1999; Engwall and Söderlind, 2007).

More recently, Qvortrup has himself commented on the epistemological emphases of some research traditions in a paper that focused on how macro work can help reveal the characteristics of childhoods (Qvortrup, 2008). And with colleagues he has produced a definitive collection of papers on childhood, drawing together contributions from many traditions and several societies: *The Palgrave Handbook of Childhood Studies* (Qvortup *et al.*, 2009).

Section 5: Current UK work on the sociology of childhood

As indicated, I think that much of the precursor work came out in the USA. But much of the theoretical development took place in Germany and through the analyses carried out by Qvortrup and his colleagues. Work in the UK has included many empirical studies. One reason for this has been the continued interest in childhood by non-governmental organizations (NGOs) – perhaps in part because they argued that childhood was widely regarded as a social problem. Another reason is the concern felt by many researchers – both in NGOs and in universities – that children's rights and welfare have been poorly served by successive UK governments. In both cases, 'listening to children's voices' has been seen as a key way into better understanding. It is fair to say that social constructionism and links between sociological and rights concerns have been interwoven in the UK research work.

An important factor leading to a spurt of empirical studies with children in the late 1990s in the UK was the funding by the Economic and Social Research Council (ESRC) of a programme of studies ('Children 5–16'), which, as the brief stated, should focus on the child as social actor. Reasons for commissioning such a programme are no doubt complex. It may be that, again, the idea that childhood was in crisis was a spur. Child poverty had risen dramatically during 18 years of Conservative government and (in response) the demonization of childhood by both politicians and the media was in full swing (for discussion, see Pilcher and Wagg, 1996). Indeed, the charities working for children (and there are more of these in the UK than anywhere else) were articulate not only in documenting the miseries of childhood, but perhaps more importantly in speaking up for children's interests and rights. The 22 studies funded on the Children 5–16 ESRC programme mostly did put children centre stage as social actors, and gave prominence to 'children's voices'. RoutledgeFalmer published a series of books (2001–3) with the general title The Future of Childhood, drawing on these ESRC-funded studies and others, and organized under topics: child–adult relations; work; home and school; the impacts of technological change; city and rural life; and changes in families (Alanen and Mayall, 2001; Mizen *et al.*, 2001; Edwards, 2002; Hutchby and Moran-Ellis, 2001; Christensen and O'Brien, 2003; Jensen and McKee, 2003).

A second reason for both the ESRC's commissioning of a programme of work on childhood and the more general popularity in the UK of empirical studies with and for children relates to the UNCRC. Since the emergence of the UNCRC (1989), UK governments have been slow to implement it (see Lansdown, 1994), and much work on, with and for children has taken on a political slant in the UK, with researchers blending the 'voices of children' with rights-oriented commentary and recommendations. This trend towards work arising from the UNCRC has been noticed in some other European countries (see section 6), but less so in others, which may reflect researchers' satisfaction with their government's implementation of the UNCRC, or less critical views of their society in general, or national traditions shaping the focus of research – for instance on education.

An important development, notably in the UK, in the last 15 years or so, has been work on methods of research with and for children, and – a closely related topic – on the ethics of carrying out research with and for children (e.g. Christensen and James, 2000; Alderson and Morrow, 2004, 2011; Greene and Hogan, 2005). This development can be seen as complementary to the experiences researchers have had in carrying out the many empirical studies of children and childhood and the ethical issues raised by the UNCRC. This development can also be seen as a response to the proliferation of childhood studies courses at universities, many of which require students to undertake empirical research. As regards methods, a key topic has been whether and how to ensure children's participation at all stages of a research study:

planning, data collection, analysis and dissemination. Others have tried out varied methods of data collection within a research study, with a view to finding successful ways of engaging with, especially, younger children: 'the mosaic approach' and to triangulating the data (e.g. Clark and Moss, 2001). A central topic has been how to respond to the undoubted power imbalance between children and adults within a study. In an early consideration of this topic Mandell (1991) argued that the researcher might adopt a 'least adult role', where he or she works to be accepted as part of the children's daily experience and activities. This was the approach adopted by Corsaro in his participant research in childcare centres (1997: 29–30). However, others argued that though one might seek to defuse or soften adult power, children were unlikely to be fooled by 'least adult' tactics, and furthermore that the researcher, in the last analysis, exercised power in interpretation and dissemination (Mayall, 1994). Since those early days, ideas about adult and child participation in research projects have moved on. Punch (2002), for instance, has provided a thorough discussion of methods, and some pioneers have enabled children to act as researchers. Thus they have acted as advocates for children, providing the means for children to carry out all stages of a project, from designing the research questions to disseminating the results and working for policy change (e.g. CESESMA, 2012).

The interlinked topic of the ethics of research with children has also attracted important work, exploring all stages of research: design, recruitment, consent, empirical methods, analysis, writing up, and dissemination. Ethical guidelines are now issued by education, psychology, and sociology professional and research associations, and while much of this work has been done in the minority world, discussions of ethical issues have been set out by and for researchers in the majority world, where researchers are often engaged on sensitive investigations into, for instance, the views of child sex workers about their work, and children's experiences of AIDS (e.g. Boyden and Ennew, 2007; Ansell and Van Blerk, 2005; Schenk and Williamson, 2005; Montgomery, 2007; Adebe, 2009; Morrow, 2009). The authors of the 2011 third edition of their work, *The Ethics of Research with Children and Young People* (Alderson and Morrow, 2011) note 'welcome growth' since 2004 in research and consultation with children, in a wide range of methods, lessons learned from research by NGOs and in other countries, the establishment of ethics committees, and training about ethics for social researchers (138). This growth is reflected in the long list of references they give. Their book sets out ethical issues arising in the ten main stages of a research study: planning the research; assessing harms and benefits; respect for rights, privacy, and confidentiality; research design; funding; ethics committees; information giving and consent in the data collecting stage; dissemination; and the impacts on children. They address basic issues such as: Is the research worth doing? Will it do harm or bring benefits? They end by emphasizing that individuals alone cannot solve all questions; it is necessary for societies to establish research ethics committees and work towards national agreements on social research ethics.

Children's status, rights, and competence

Sociological, psychological, and international research about children[3] has investigated their competence and rights. Former research emphasized normative assessments of child competence, and relied on laboratory conditions, standardized tests, adults' accounts, and statistical analysis. More recent research has investigated children's own views, experiences, and reasoning in the context of their everyday lives and relationships. Researchers have found higher levels than were formerly supposed possible of children's competencies: social competence (Hutchby and Moran Ellis, 1998); early relationships and moral reasoning and responses (Mayall, 2002; Dunn, 2004); technical competence and sophisticated understanding of the mass media (Hutchby and Moran Ellis, 2001; Buckingham, 2003); economic and work competencies in homes, streets, markets, agriculture, and industry in the minority world and particularly in the majority world (Morrow, 1994; Mizen, Pole and Boulton, 2001; Ennew, 2002; Morrow, 2003; Liebel, 2004; Katz, 2004; Lansdown, 2006; Boyden and Ennew, 2007); children's early political understanding (Khan, 1997; Butler, 1998; Connolly, Smith, and Kelly, 2002); their agency when working with NGOs and local and national government (Hart, 1992; Hood, 2002, 2004); their work as learners and teachers (Gardner, 1993; John, 2004); and their participation in research and evaluations (Willow *et al.*, 2004; Christensen and James, 2007) and in complex personal decision making (Alderson, 1993; Alderson and Goodey, 1998; Neale, 2002; Thomas, 2002; Alderson, Sutcliffe, and Curtis, 2006).

The wealth of relatively new empirical evidence from the sociology of childhood challenges, but also in some cases expands, findings from older research on child competencies (for example, on babies' agency in Stern, 1977; Als, 1999; Murray and Andrews, 2000; Alderson, Hawthorne, and Killen, 2005; Alderson, 2008). Childhood research theories, methods, and analysis, as much as the research data, can reveal children's competencies. Also revealed are the effects of expectations and contexts on perceptions and performance, and on the social construction and reconstruction of child competence (or incompetence and vulnerability: see Katz, 2005). Much of the

---

[3] Priscilla Alderson has contributed the next two paragraphs.

research involves children as agents and partners, and publicizes their views and voices. Feminists challenged patriarchal concepts of 'man's' personhood, citizenship, and rights on the grounds that women are entitled to equal rights. The evidence of early child competence, as well as international surveys of children's suffering (UNICEF, 2007), support the view that children too are persons *now*, not merely *future* beings, and that they are therefore entitled to 'recognition of the inherent dignity and of the equal and inalienable rights of all members of the human family [as] the foundation of freedom, justice, and peace in the world' (UN, 1989: preamble). The sociology of childhood and of children's competence, status, and rights will, potentially, contribute greatly to informing policies and practices that affect children across the world.

So discussions about children as citizens have benefited from feminist work, which has challenged sharp distinctions between being and not being a citizen and has suggested more multi-layered concepts, which pay attention to the variations between groups of people in their power to participate and at what levels, including both the 'private' and 'public' domains (e.g. Lister, 2007). Lister argues that less powerful people (which would include women and children) can be understood as citizens by virtue of their rights. Further, both women and children can be understood as contributing citizens through their people work in the 'private' domain. These arguments have been further considered in Susie Weller's work on how young people participate in community development (2007).

Childhood embodiment

Early work in the sociology of childhood focused on children's agency, some of it within social constructionist approaches and on children as a social group. In both cases, the work stressed the social and, it has been argued more recently, downplayed an essential element in children's experiences and in child–adult relations. For clearly, as every mother knows, adults' relations with children, especially with young children, are embodied relations. As with some other developments in studying children, feminism has been one inspiration in pointing to how women manage their bodies and how women's bodies are understood and manipulated, physically, morally, and socially, as they move between homes and jobs, the private and the public (Martin, 1989). Similarly, studies have pointed to how children's bodies are understood, managed and demoted in schools, and how children's own embodied experiences differ at home and at school. Thus it has been found that children receive more holistic care at home, with attention to their bodies, minds, and emotions; whereas at school, while teachers may be kindly, the formal agenda of school focuses on the academic and the informal agenda on (often unspoken) norms of school behaviour, and may somewhat devalue children's wishes to control their own bodies and to be active (e.g. Waksler, 1996; Mayall, 1998; Foley, 2001). Alan Prout's 2000 book usefully assembles papers exploring, mainly from social constructionist viewpoints, the embodied child's experiences and adult–child embodied relations across time. In these enterprises, a promising line for theoretical development is provided by Bourdieu, whose analyses of embodied social interactions in *Distinction* (1986) can be seen as a basis for reconsidering child–adult negotiations in both homes and schools. A further topic for allied research that could benefit from further development is in the area of the sociology of the emotions (Bendelow and Williams, 1998), again drawing on feminist work carried out, notably by Arlie Hochschild (e.g. 1998). Here we are concerned with how people manage their feelings in the varying social (including institutional) environments where they find themselves. As regards children, the emotional and intellectual journeys made by dying children in a hospice and how they used their knowledge to foster good child–parent relations were the focus of an important study by Myra Bluebond-Langner (1978). And children's embodied experience, this time with a particular emphasis on feeling and why it matters, has been explored across the home and school (Mayall, 1998; Bendelow and Mayall, 2000).

Children and the media

For some time the study of the relations between children and the media remained on the edges of the sociology of childhood.[4] Early thinking in mainstream media research focused on examinations of the text and the ideological power of the mass media on society on the one hand, and individual effects on emotion and behaviour on the other, drawing on psychological behavioural models. Concerns were also expressed about the fact that the media gave children a window on the 'adult world' that might be inappropriate (Postman, 1982). The potentially corrupting effects of violence and sexual content have been uppermost, and early research in this area set out to challenge a simplistic notion of modality that this implied (Hodge and Tripp, 1986). Notoriously, the Bulger murder in 1993 in the UK became the centre of heated debate (Barker and Petley, 1997; see also Jenks, 1996). One feature of this debate was the contrast drawn between the UK response and the societal responses to similar events in Norway at the same time, demonstrating differing dominant conceptualizations of childhood and society. Whereas in Norway the children who injured a child and left her to die remained in their school and their community, in England the children who killed a child were tried, convicted, and sent to be contained

---

[4] Liesbeth de Block has contributed this paragraph.

in secure accommodation. Questions of the role of media in everyday lives and social relationships became prominent in the 1990s and coincided with the increased focus on children's agency and the development of a new sociology of childhood. Research emerged demonstrating the ways in which children might use media in the negotiation of peer and generational power relationships (Buckingham, 2000) and simply for enjoyment (Buckingham, 1996)! Again much of this research has remained in the minority world, but this is changing. New areas of research have followed the developments of new communication technologies with increased interest in global media (Wasko *et al.*, 2001; de Block and Buckingham, 2007), the internet and social networking (Livingstone, 2002; Holloway and Valentine, 2003) and video games (Cassell and Jenkins, 1998). However, with each new technological development, old and often contradictory concerns and public panics arise about how media might be corrupting an innocent childhood on the one hand or how it is highlighting a potential for evil that needs to be monitored and tamed on the other. A powerful notion, both romanticized and feared (Tapscott, 2008; Buckingham and Willett, 2006), of the media-savvy child who is born with computer knowledge superior to that of an adult and therefore with great power, is central to continuing research and concern in this area (Livingstone *et al.*, 2011). Finally, it is interesting that these new developments have also allowed research in the sociology of childhood a greater cross-disciplinary possibility with research in anthropology, social geography, digital technology, social psychology and education.

Globalization

Globalization has been referred to earlier, for instance, in connection with the export of minority world psychological descriptions of childhood. But as scholars have observed, the notion of one-directional flow – from minority to majority – does not match the reality of what is taking place. By globalization, at least in respect of children and childhood, scholars nowadays tend to refer to three intersecting trends (e.g. de Block and Buckingham, 2007; Wells, 2009). The first trend is processes whereby a society is exposed to economic, political, and social forces from outside, which change the conditions of life in the society (e.g. Kaufman and Rizzini, 2002). A very clear instance is how the minority world understanding that the proper place for children is in school has infiltrated other societies, not least with the expressed aim of helping children to compete in global markets. But the traditional ways of living childhoods, where children contribute to the household and national division of labour, often come into conflict with this minority world understanding. Research studies in varying societies have sought to explore children's own perceptions of the place of productive work in their lives (e.g. Woodhead, 1999), and to explore what the factors are that lead to children not attending the schools provided (e.g. Liebel *et al.*, 2012). Cindy Katz (2004) showed the impacts of globalization on children growing up in an area of the Sudan and an area of New York. An example of how external pressures may alter (for the worse) conditions of life is also exemplified by minority world views on schooling: when the United States banned the sale of goods made by people under the age of 15, the children were sacked from that employment, but went, not to school, but to more dangerous jobs (Kaufmann and Rizzini, 2002: 7). However, it may also be argued that political change – towards the development of democratic governments – can bring benefits. Thus the social status of childhood can be raised, where children are regarded not as their parents' possessions but as citizens of their state, a process aided by attention to the United Nations' focus on children's welfare and rights.

The second trend is the international influence of documents that present particular visions, or constructions, of childhood, and operate, whether purposefully or less so, to normalize these visions. Since these documents are mostly drawn up by minority world lawyers and other scholars, they tend to rely on and promote minority world visions. Important among these documents and the accompanying processes are the UNCRC, UNICEF, and the International Labour Organization (ILO). Jo Boyden (1997) argues that the UNCRC in particular has been very influential across the world. International monitoring of its implementation by the UN Committee has led to benefits: the increased visibility of, for instance, the exploitation of children as soldiers and as sex workers. On the other hand, she notes downsides: the spread of internationally competitive education systems can be described as promoting the exploitation of children in schools, where they are forced to engage in stressful work. These international pronouncements and sets of guidance can be seen to have stirred up controversies about the relative priority that should be given to schooling and to productive work, with the ILO, in particular, seeking to end 'child employment' worldwide. It may also be argued that the notion of the child as, above all, to be protected, rather than encouraged to participate in social worlds, is another kind of export. Sharon Stephens (1994) argues that whilst international children's rights discourses are appropriately invoked, for instance when children's lives are in danger, yet universalizing modernist discourses on childhood and children should be used only flexibly and in relation to local beliefs and practices. This is an argument developed, for instance, in Rachel Burr's (2002) analysis of the character and quality of children's lives in Vietnam in relation to the values and practices of international aid workers. The historical legacy of colonial education policies on how Calcutta children talk about their lives is analysed by Sarada Balagopalan (2002). And the development of working children's movements is discussed by Olga Nieuwenhuys (2009), who argues that children value their economic contributions, and that children and families across the world should be offered ways for children to combine their economic responsibilities with their rights to schooling (see also Liebel, Overwien, and Recknagel, 2001).

The third kind of impact of a globalized world is that it encourages the movement of people across the world, both within and across national boundaries. Migration is a central theme here, for it impacts on peer cultures, education, aspirations, and child–parent relations. As far as children are specifically concerned, such movements may be as migrants, with or without adults, to seek better means of subsistence; they may move as refugees or as asylum seekers, again, with or without adults; and they may be moved in early childhood to be adopted by adults in, generally, wealthier nations. An important research project in California has studied migration from mainly Mexico into the USA, and the parts played by children in settling into the new country and helping their parents to do so, for instance by working as advocates and translators. Children's legitimized status within the US education system also helps to introduce parents to an important social institution and provides possibilities for children to work towards a brighter future, thus modifying the character of intergenerational relations (Orellana, 2001, 2011).

In relation to the topics of this book, we may note a fourth trend, which again intersects with the other three and is touched on in the preceding three paragraphs. This is that scholarly work on childhood is not only being exported from minority world countries to majority world countries, but it is also being undertaken by local, as well as international, researchers in those majority world countries. Furthermore, research work from across the world is now appearing in research journals and researchers from across the world are meeting at conferences (including tele-conferences) and through the proliferation of university courses relating to childhood. These meetings are generating useful sets of reflections about similarities and differences between childhoods across the world, as discussed for instance by Robson, Panelli, and Punch (2007) in their consideration of rural childhoods. An interesting and important example of collaboration across societies is provided by the Young Lives study, a longitudinal study of children growing up in areas of India, Peru, Ethiopia, and Vietnam, where UK-based researchers are working with local research teams to collect and analyse macro-level and micro-level data (e.g. Morrow and Pells, 2012).

In this connection, scholars have drawn attention to the importance of adequate research methods for investigating children's lives and their social and political status. This too is a globalizing enterprise, and one where there can be give and take across the world, since research methods and the ethics of research may, on the one hand, be transferable to other contexts, and on the other may be ones particularly suited to the local, while simultaneously having lessons for those researching elsewhere. For instance, the research done with children living on the streets in a particular city may have a local character, since it will take account of the particular social institutions (such as education and care facilities locally) and of the particular factors affecting children's choice or necessity to live on the street. But it will have lessons to teach researchers in other societies about how to work respectfully with children, and how to take account of local traditions and expectations. From a conceptual point of view, research studies with street children in one society and with children who congregate in shopping malls in another (Matthews, 2003) have pointers towards considering just what the social status of children in public space is. Similarly, the fact that across the world most children make direct economic contributions to households and the nation gives very serious pause for thought to those who want UK children to spend more years in formal schooling.

As noted above, there are significant challenges posed to minority world scholars by researchers and policy-makers in the majority world. The growth of social science courses on childhood in minority world countries has brought students from across the world into contact with each other, and is allowing for interchange of ideas and knowledge. Recent conferences and seminar series in the UK have provided forums for discussion of what we can learn from each other. Notably discussion has focused on the UNCRC and its limitations in African contexts, where children's responsibilities to family and community are recognized and emphasized in the African Charter on Children's Rights, but not in the UNCRC. The experiential knowledge and expertise of working children in most of the world's countries has been an important theme for researchers, and possible conflicts with the UNCRC's prioritizing of schooling over 'work' (see article 32) have been discussed. Yet the United Nations is in no doubt that children's place is in school, and that the 'internationally agreed millennium development goal that all children should complete primary school by 2015' must be adhered to (*Guardian*, 29 October 2012, 22). The questions, What do we mean by education? and What is a child? are also raised by these topics; for interrelations and inconsistencies between 'education' and 'schooling' and childhood as status rather than as age-related have to be considered. Pioneering work on childhoods across the world was carried out by Sharon Stephens (1995), and her work is discussed and celebrated in a special edition of *Childhood* (2002, vol 9, no 1), edited by Judith Ennew and Virginia Morrow (2002). University-based courses on childhood as an international phenomenon are now established in the UK (see Wells, 2009 and Montgomery, 2008).

Childhood geographies

Researchers within the disciplines of geography have interested themselves in sociological approaches to childhood, and they too have added to knowledge about children's lives and status in societies across the world (e.g. Aitken, 2001; Holt, 2011; Kraftl, Horton, and Tucker, 2012). Geographers have contributed to the development of concepts in a number of ways, as are clearly summarized by Holloway and Valentine (2000). First, they have added to explorations of varying childhoods by examining a key factor: place. In particular, they have described how childhoods in many majority world societies, in contrast to childhoods in minority world societies, are structured by ideas of children as workers, contributors, and carers. Second, geographers, among others, have focused on the everyday spaces of childhoods: the home, the school, and the city, and have explored how each, through varying measures, controls and regulates children's bodies and minds. Children's access to streets, playspaces, and other public places has been studied (see Matthews and Smith, 2000). Third, work has focused on ideologies of, for instance, the home, rural spaces, national identity, and how understandings of these have helped to shape childhoods. Thus, for instance, according to some commentators, the home should be seen not just as the place where children *do* spend time, but where they *should* spend time. The notion of a country childhood as an ideal, where children play freely, in contact with nature and out of the immediate supervision of adults, has gained currency in some societies, and notably through the stories told for English children – such as *Swallows and Amazons* (Arthur Ransome, 1930). It can be argued that the more time children spend exploring new technologies, the less time they can and will give to interactions with the natural world, with consequent loss of knowledge and identity.

It can be seen that these interesting explorations of childhoods fall broadly within social constructionist understandings of the shaping of childhoods. Finally on this, the journal *Children's Geographies* has pioneered work relating the character of childhoods to varying social and historical forces in varying societies, and exploring how majority and minority world societies and researchers can learn from each other to improve the study of childhood (see for instance *Children's Geographies*, 10 (3), August 2012).

Section 6: Other recent developments

In recent years, many societies have developed work on the sociology of childhood, held conferences, and produced books of papers. A useful set of papers from ten countries describes the history of and current state of play in sociological approaches to childhood (*Current Sociology*, 2010: 58): Finland, the UK, Brazil, Australia, France, Italy, Germany, Romania, the USA, and the Netherlands. In this section I draw on some of these reports (but I note that for more detail readers should consult them directly). Each of these countries derives its particular interests in childhood from its specific social, political, and intellectual history; and it has been observed, for instance for Australia, that studies in English, from the UK and Nordic countries, have been influential in establishing bases for further development (Van Krieken, 2010). Another common strand across these country reports is the importance of the UNCRC in promoting discussion, policies, and research on children's social and political status in each society.

The widening of the field of the sociology of childhood took place in many countries during the 1990s, as is detailed, for instance by Régine Sirota (2010) in respect of France and other French-speaking nations. A Francophone sociology of childhood group has held annual conferences (Sirota, 2006; Brougère *et al.*, 2008); this brings together French, Belgian, Canadian, and some South American countries. In France, the sociology of education has been the main site of research about children and childhood, with traditional emphasis on children as socialization projects, but Régine Sirota became interested in children's own agency, and she began to engage with international networks of childhood sociology researchers (Sirota, 1998). Cléopâtre Montandon, whose background was in anthropology, also joined an international working group to reconsider child–adult relations (Montandon, 2001). An interesting development has been the study of intergenerational relations, with a particular focus on families who migrate (for instance, Attias-Donfut and Segalen, 1998). The strength of theoretical sociological work in France has been harnessed to consider the application of, for instance, Bourdieu and Boltanski to the study of childhood (Garnier, 1995).

Another example of how interest in sociological approaches to childhood is strengthened through linguistic links is provided by commentaries on work in Portuguese. In Portugal, the sociology of childhood is a developing field. An Institute of Child Studies has been started at the University of Minho at Braga, and acts as a centre for the development of the discipline. It has established links with other universities: Oporto, Aveiro, Lisbon, and others. It offers, since 1999, a master's degree in the sociology of childhood. International networks have also been established, especially with Brazil, where some publications in Portuguese have begun to appear.[5] Work on childhood emerged out of concern for social-class-related concerns – about street children and children as criminals – but also out of established work on children and schooling. The UNCRC has also raised the profile of children as social actors, with rights (Castro and Kosminsky, 2010). Topics for study have included: children's work, education (0–12), children's identity, and citizenship. The work in French and Portuguese helps to link up the geographic and scholarly worlds, so that South American countries are now involved in international networks with European scholars.

Whilst language can bring national traditions together and promote international comparisons, it can also act as a barrier. I noted earlier how fundamental German research from the 1980s onwards was not well known in English-speaking countries. Another good example comes from Romania, where the country report author, Stanciulescu (2010), notes the development in the 1930s and 1940s of a structural sociological approach to childhood at the University of Bucharest School of Sociology. Researchers studied the concrete 'social unities' that shaped the character of childhoods. One line of research concerned how the social worlds of childhood mirrored the social structures of their society. However, after the Second World War under the communist regime (to 1989), other topics were to be addressed by sociologists – industrialization, urbanization, and modernization – so this important strand of research was abandoned. Since 1989, children in difficulty and children at risk, or as risk-takers, and marginalized children (Roma, street children) have been the focus of research by social workers and psychologists. It seems that the pioneering work at Bucharest had to be done all over again in the Nordic countries and Germany from the 1980s onwards.

Other more diverse factors are held to account for the status of the sociology of childhood in some countries, and for some countries, factors remain obscure. In Finland, as in some other societies, it has been children as objects of education that have provided one springboard for sociological work, and more recently the UNCRC has pointed towards work on children's rights (see Strandell, 2010). It is undoubtedly also the work of one determined researcher, Leena Alanen, that has been important both nationally and internationally in considering intersections of the micro and macro, and in promoting childhood research work in Finnish universities. As regards the USA, I traced earlier on the dominance of psychological approaches to childhood there; Loretta Bass (2010) provides a further analysis, pointing to

---

[5] Catarina Tomas, personal communication.

the multidisciplinary character of some emerging research centres. Two other countries that have had surprisingly little sociological work on childhood are Italy and the Netherlands. Baraldi (2010) argues that the 1990s political work in Italy on children's citizenship and participation has 'evaporated'; he sees 'lukewarm interest within the sociological community' as an important factor underlying the slow progress of sociological work. Rineke van Daalen (2010), in her country report on the Netherlands, refers to social changes: changes in family structures, and new tensions in the balance of state and parental responsibility for children. She suggests that study of the social problems of children rather than sociological study has been the focus of work on childhood. She also points to other traditions of work on childhood: in anthropology and in history. In the end, why some lines of enquiry emerge in a society and others do not is indeed hard to disentangle!

Concluding discussion

Perhaps I should stress here again why it is important to give sociological attention to childhood. Essentially it is because a proper account of how society works has to include all its constituent members: the varying social groups that make up society. Just as feminism demonstrated that an account of society that omitted, distorted, or devalued women's contributions and experiences was inadequate, the same is true of children as a social group. It is necessary to consider how – and how far – childhood constitutes part of the social structure of societies, and how children participate in helping to maintain and promote societies through their economic contributions and relational processes (for recent discussion, see Qvortrup, 2009). These theoretical investigations about children's contributions give emphasis to children as people who should be valued as people: who participate, join in, have relevant knowledge, and experience to contribute. This is also a rights-related and practice-oriented point: children will feel valued only if they can contribute to societal well-being, and if their contributions are recognized and valued.

These ways of thinking about children and childhood are somewhat different from those of developmental psychology, which, though it has changed in the last 30 years, retains some specific focuses that differentiate it from sociological approaches. Thus psychology continues to focus on the journey children make towards adulthood (the gold standard!); on the individual; and on deviations from normal development requiring interventions to restore children to normality. Though it has become more aware of social context, it still lacks a fully interactive set of theories to consider agency and structure, and it lacks thorough attention to the politics of childhood.

However, there is a current move to argue that, whilst emphasis on children as beings and as people is important, perhaps we should be bringing together the two key disciplines that have interested themselves in children: developmental psychology and the sociology of childhood. Nick Lee (2001) argues that we all develop throughout life, and so we scholars should include development in intersection with personhood (put 'becoming' and 'being' into fruitful interrelations). Another related argument is based on the point that children do, demonstrably, develop during their journey to adulthood. Woodhead (2009) argues that since immaturity is one of the most distinctive features of young humans, this immaturity and the bodily, emotional, and intellectual changes that take place along the path of childhood must form a part of the considerations people make when trying to understand and provide for children (see also for discussion Aitken, 2001). Thus, for instance, respecting children's participation rights in line with the UNCRC requires considering how to adapt practices to children's maturity and understanding, their 'evolving capacities' (UNCRC, article 12). These are very interesting points of view and their value depends partly on what one thinks the enterprise of studying childhood is about, what it aims at, and what the usefulness of sociological approaches to childhood is. My view is that studying childhood is about describing the character and status of childhood, and advancing arguments in favour of improving its character and status. If sociology is the study of social systems, about how social groups interrelate and how the social order works, with due attention to power issues, then the focus as regards children and childhood has to be as it is for adults and adulthood – a central focus on the social. The adult designation of some people as children, with accompanying adult ideas about what children are, and accompanying institutional arrangements for children, is what will concern us most, not how far along the road to adulthood, in psychological terms, they have come – and have to go. Yet this argument too can be countered, as above, by arguing that we adults will do best by children if we take due account of development in intersection with social intergenerational relations.

Alan Prout (2005) also argues that we should put together all the kinds of knowledge we have about children and childhood and consider the intersections of this knowledge. In particular, he argues that childhood sociologists have worked through the dichotomies between psychology and sociology for long enough (e.g. becoming versus being; incompetence versus competence; future-oriented versus present-oriented; individual versus group) and it is time to consider how to work with both streams of knowledge as well as with a range of theoretical approaches, including actor network theory (see also for discussion James, 2010). I note here that many of the courses on childhood in UK universities and colleges have followed this route; they are multidisciplinary or interdisciplinary, and are often called Childhood Studies courses. To take one important example, the Open University BA Childhood course (U212) sets out its aims: 'To span conventional academic boundaries in order to achieve a more interdisciplinary understanding, as well as to acknowledge the unresolved tensions between different approaches to childhood' (Montgomery and Woodhead, 2003: ix). One point to be made about this aim is that differing disciplines put varying emphasis on ontology, and therefore how to reconcile these varying emphases is a central task to be faced. Thus, by long tradition, sociology has insisted on the social, economic, institutional 'facts' out there, how these structure people's lives, and how human agents interact with these structures. These basic ideas have survived social constructionist and post-modernist fashions in sociology (in the second half of the twentieth century), which placed more emphasis on epistemology (what we know and how we know it). Psychology has aimed for truth, universally true, but since at least the 1970s psychology as story-telling to suit local contexts has been seen as a more appropriate stance. Currently, developmental psychology can be understood as concerned with the social construction of childhood. Furthermore, a clear, thorough understanding of sociological concepts is important in order to combat the detrimental effects that simplistic interpretations of developmental psychology (especially as they serve to guide education policy and practice) continue to have on children's lives, not just in its cruder traditional forms, but by its emphasis on normality, stages, outcomes, incompetence, vulnerability, and individuality. Sociology can be seen to have a discrete function in proposing other ways of understanding children: as agents in the present tense, as competent and as a social group. Sociology also presents potentially useful challenges to adults in proposing the crucial importance of processes within intergenerational relations, as structuring childhoods, and how they are lived and experienced. So an ongoing question to address is whether the point that sociology and psychology have differing concerns and ask differing questions allows for joint work. For those of us who regard the sociology of childhood as essentially a political enterprise (as outlined in the introduction), it is important to harness the tools and methods of sociology in the work towards raising the status of childhood in societies.

With this aim in mind, I note that there are some very promising sociological lines of enquiry being pursued using the work of some respected theorists. Thus, for instance, Priscilla Alderson has been working on a book focusing on childhood through the lens of the critical realism movement, led by Roy Bhaskar (Alderson, 2013). There is a growing and substantial array of research papers that draw on Bourdieu's relational sociology to consider childhood and specifically child–adult relations (e.g. Connolly, 2000; Haines, 2003; Ingram, 2009). Leena Alanen (2009) has continued to build on Mannheim's understanding of generation in order to develop ideas about intergenerational relations. She and colleagues have also drawn on the work of Bourdieu to consider fields in which children and adults negotiate the status of their knowledge and the character of childhood (Alanen, 2011; Siisiäinen and Alanen, 2011). Heinz Hengst (2009) too draws on Mannheim and discusses interrelations between his ideas about how and when people process experience into knowledge, and Bourdieu's concept of habitus: the settled sets of understandings acquired early in life. In particular he explores how far 'consumer children' or 'media children' can be said to constitute a generation.

Finally, I flag up the point that there seems to be some movement towards the acceptance by mainstream sociology of its junior member. When I was writing my 2002 book, I checked UK basic course books on sociology to see if they mentioned childhood. They did, but only under the headings 'childcare', 'child development' and 'child abuse'; also 'see parenting' and 'see socialization'. That is, the topics chosen were predominantly about adult concerns, rather than focusing on childhood as a study in its own right. Ten years on, childhood viewed through sociological spectacles can be found in some textbooks (e.g. Marsh *et al.*, 2009) and aspects of childhood within broadly sociological approaches are studied for A-level sociology at school. For instance Webb *et al.* (2004) focus on the social construction of childhood and the quality of childhoods across the world. Furthermore, whilst there are some journals (*Childhood, Children's Geographies* and *Children and Society*) that specialize in work on childhood, mainstream sociology journals (such as the *British Journal of Sociology* and *Sociology*) now also carry papers on childhood, drawing on sociological approaches and understandings. For this country, then, there has been some movement, whilst as indicated earlier, societies vary in the status and salience of sociological approaches to childhood.

In sum, my view is that sociological work on childhood and for children is an important enterprise, in order to study and to raise the status of childhoods in varying societies. While this may be a long journey, with many setbacks and some doubting commentators, it has to be undertaken patiently and thoroughly. The analogy with feminism holds: since the early 1970s, women have faced a huge task and, many may argue, feminism has nowhere near reached its goals, yet it remains active and committed. Sociological approaches to childhood, it can be argued, face even greater difficulties. However, some progress has been made and more can be achieved.

References

Adebe, T. (2009) 'Multiple methods, complex dilemmas: Negotiating socio-ethical spaces in participatory research with disadvantaged children'. *Children's Geographies*, 7 (4), 451–65.

Aitken, S. (2001) *Geographies of Young People: The morally contested spaces of identity*. London: Routledge.

Alanen, L. (1992) 'Modern childhood? Exploring the "child question" in sociology'. Research Report 50. Finland: University of Jyväskylä.

— (1994) 'Gender and generation: Feminism and the "child question"'. In J. Qvortrup, M. Bardy, G. Sgritta and H. Wintersberger (eds), *Childhood Matters: Social theory, practice and politics*. Aldershot: Avebury Press.

— (2003) 'Childhoods: The generational ordering of social relations'. In B. Mayall and H. Zeiher (eds), *Childhood in Generational Perspective*. London: Institute of Education.

— (2009) 'Generational order'. In J. Qvortrup, W. A. Corsaro, and M.S. Honig (eds), *The Palgrave Handbook of Childhood Studies*. London: Palgrave Macmillan.

— (2011) 'Moving towards a relational sociology of childhood'. In R. Braches-Chyrek, C. Röhner, A. Schaarschuch and H. Sünker (eds), *Kindheiten Gesellschaften: Interdiziplinare Zugänge zur Kindheitsforschung*. Opladen: Barbara Budrich Verläg.

Alanen, L. and Mayall, B. (eds) (2001) *Conceptualising Child–Adult Relations*. London: RoutledgeFalmer.

Alderson, P. (1993) *Children's Consent to Surgery*. Buckingham: Open University Press.

— (2000) *Young Children's Rights*. London: Jessica Kingsley Publishers.

— (2008) *A Sourcebook of the Youngest Children's Rights*. London: Jessica Kingsley/Save the Children.

— (2013) *Childhoods Real and Imagined*, vol. 1: *An introduction to critical realism and childhood studies*. London: Routledge.

Alderson, P. and Goodey, C. (1998) *Enabling Education: Experiences in special and ordinary schools*. London: Tufnell Press.

Alderson, P., Hawthorne, J., and Killen, M. (2005) 'The participation rights of premature babies'. *International Journal of Children's Rights*, 13, 31–50.

Alderson, P. and Morrow, V. (2011) *The Ethics of Research with Children and Young People: A practical handbook*. London: Sage. First edition published in 1995 and again in 2004, by Barnardos.

Alderson, P., Sutcliffe, K. and Curtis, K. (2006) 'Children's consent to medical treatment'. *Hastings Center Report*, 36 (6), 25–34.

Allport, G. (1968) 'The historical background of modern social psychology'. In G. Lindzey and E. Aronson (eds), *The Handbook of Social Psychology*. Second edition. New York: Addison-Wesley.

Als, H. (1999) 'Reading the premature infant'. In E. Goldson (ed.), *Developmental Interventions in the Neonatal Intensive Care Nursery*. New York: Oxford University Press.

Ambert, A.M. (1986) 'Sociology of sociology: The place of children in North American sociology'. *Sociological Studies of Child Development*, 1 (1), 11–31.

Ansell, N. and Van Blerk, L. (2005) 'Joining the conspiracy? Negotiating ethics and emotions in researching around AIDS in Southern Africa'. *Ethics, Place and Environment*, 8 (1), 61–82.

Ariès, P. (1962) *Centuries of Childhood*. Harmondsworth: Penguin.

Armstrong, D. (1983) *The Political Anatomy of the Body: Medical knowledge in Britain in the twentieth century*. Cambridge: Cambridge University Press.

Attias-Donfut, C. and Segalen, M. (1998) *Grandparents: La famille à travers les generations*. Paris: Editions Odile Jacob.

Balagopalan, S. (2002) 'Constructing indigenous childhoods: Colonialism, vocational education and the working child'. *Childhood*, 9 (1), 19–34.

Baldwin, A. (1967) *Theories of Child Development*. London: John Wiley.

Baraldi, C. (2010) 'Children's citizenships: Limitations and possibilities of childhood sociology'. *Current Sociology*, 58 (2), 272–91.

Barker, M. and Petley, J. (1997) *Ill Effects: The media/violence debate*. London: Routledge.

Bass, L. (2010) 'Childhood in sociology and society: The US perspective'. *Current Sociology*, 58 (2), 335–50.

Becker, H. (1963) *Outsiders: Studies in the sociology of deviance*. New York: Free Press of Glencoe.

— (ed.) (1967) *The Other Side: Perspectives on deviance*. New York: Free Press of Glencoe.

Bendelow, G. and Mayall, B. (2000) 'How children manage emotion in schools'. In S. Fineman (ed.), *Emotions in Organizations*. London: Sage.

Bendelow, G. and Williams, S.J. (1998) 'Introduction: Emotions in social life: mapping the sociological terrain'. In G. Bendelow and S.J. Williams (eds), *Emotions in Social Life: Critical themes and contemporary issues*. London: Routledge.

Bettelheim, B. (1971) *The Children of the Dream*. London: Paladin Books.

de Block, L. and Buckingham, D. (2007) *Global Children, Global Media: Migration, media and childhood*. London: Palgrave Macmillan.

Bluebond-Langner, M. (1978) *The Private Worlds of Dying Children*. Princeton, NJ: Princeton University Press.

Boulton, M.B. (1983) *On Being a Mother: A study of women with pre-school children*. London: Tavistock.

Bourdieu, P. (1986) *Distinction*. London: Routledge.

Boyden, J. (1997) 'Childhood and the policy makers'. In A. James and A. Prout (eds), *Constructing and Reconstructing Childhood: Contemporary issues in the sociological study of childhood*. London: Falmer Press. Second edition.

Boyden, J. and Ennew, J. (2007) *Children in Focus: A manual for participatory research with children*. Stockholm: Rädda Barnen.

Bradley, B.S. (1989) *Visions of Infancy: A critical introduction to child psychology*. Cambridge: Polity Press.

Brayfield, A. (1998) 'Academic representations of childhood: A longitudinal content analysis of *Journal of Marriage and the Family, 1939–1997*'. Unpublished paper given at ISA conference, July 1998, Montreal, Canada.

Bronfenbrenner, U. (1971) *Two Worlds of Childhood: The USA and Russia*. London: Allen and Unwin.

— (1979) *The Ecology of Human Development: Experiments by nature and design*. Cambridge, MA: Harvard University Press.

Bronfenbrenner, U., Kessel, F., Kessen, W., and White, S. (1986) 'Towards a critical social history of developmental psychology'. *American Psychologist*, 41 (11), 1218–30.

Brougère, G. (ed.) (2008) *Nouveaux Paradigmes pour Repenser l'Éducation Préscolaire*. Paris: Peter Lang.

Buckingham, D. (1996) *Moving Images: Understanding children's emotional responses to television*. Manchester: Manchester University Press.

— (2000) *After the Death of Childhood: Growing up in the age of electronic media*. Cambridge: Polity Press.

— (2003) 'Multimedia Childhoods'. In M.J. Kehily and J. Swann (eds), *Children's Cultural Worlds*. Chichester: Wiley/Open University.

Buckingham, D. and Willett, R. (eds) (2006) *Digital Generations: Children, young people and new media*. London: Lawrence Erlbaum.

Burman, E. (1994) *Deconstructing Developmental Psychology*. Second edition 2007. London: Routledge.

— (1996) 'Local, global or globalised: Child development and international child rights legislation'. *Childhood*, 3 (1), 45–66.

Burr, R. (2002) 'Global and local approaches to children's rights in Vietnam'. *Childhood*, 9 (1), 49–62.

Butler, M. (1998) 'Negotiating place: The importance of children's realities'. In S. Steinberg and J. Kincheloe (eds), *Students as Researchers: Creating classrooms that matter*. London: Falmer.

Cassell, J. and Jenkins, H. (eds) (1998) *From Barbie to Mortal Kombat: Gender and computer games* Cambridge, MA: MIT Press.

De Castro, L.R. and Kosminsky, E.V. (2010) 'Childhood and its regimes of visibility in Brazil: An analysis of the contribution of the social sciences'. *Current Sociology*, 58 (2), 206–31.

Christensen, P. and James, A. (eds) (2000) *Research with Children: Perspectives and practices*. Second edition 2008. London: Falmer Press.

Christensen, P. and O'Brien, M. (eds) (2003) *Children in the City: Home, neighbourhood and community*. London: RoutledgeFalmer.

CESESMA (Centre for Education in Health and Environment) (2012) *Learn to Live without Violence: Transformative research by children and young people*. Translated by Harry Shier. Nicaragua: CESESMA.

Clark, A. and Moss, P. (2001) *Listening to Young Children: The Mosaic Approach*. London: National Children's Bureau/Joseph Rowntree Foundation.

Clausen, J.A. (ed.) (1968) 'Chapter 2'. In J.A. Clausen (ed.) *Socialization and Society*. Boston, MA: Little Brown and Co.

Cohen, B., Moss, P., Petrie, P. and Wallace, C. (2004) *A New Deal for Children? Reforming education and care in England, Scotland and Sweden*. Bristol: Policy Press.

Cole, M. (1996) *Cultural Psychology: A once and future discipline*. Cambridge, MA and London: Harvard University Press.

Connolly, P. (2000) 'Racism and young girls' peer-group relations: The experiences of South Asian girls'. *Sociology*, 34, 499–519.

Connolly, P., Smith, A. and Kelly, B. (2002) *Too Young to Notice? The cultural and political awareness of 3–6 year olds in Northern Ireland*. Belfast: Community Relations Council.

Corsaro, W.A. (1997) *The Sociology of Childhood*. Thousand Oaks, CA: Pine Forge Press.

Craib, I. (1992) *Modern Social Theory: From Parsons to Habermas*. New York and London: Harvester Wheatsheaf.

Cunningham, H. (1991) *The Children of the Poor: Represenatations of childhood since the seventeenth century*. Oxford: Blackwell.

Danziger, K. (ed.) (1970) *Readings in Child Socialization*. Oxford: Pergamon Press.

— (1971) *Socialization*. Harmondsworth: Penguin.

Davin, A. (1990) 'When is a child not a child?' In H. Corr and L. Jamieson (eds), *Politics of Everyday Life: Continuity and change in work and the family*. London: Macmillan.

Dencik, L. (1989) 'Growing up in the post-modern age: On the child's situation in the modern family and on the position of the family in the modern welfare state'. *Acta Sociologica*, 32 (2), 155–80.

Denzin, N.K. (1977) *Child Socialization*. San Francisco: Jossey Bass.

Dunn, J. (1988) *The Beginnings of Social Understanding*. Oxford: Blackwells.

— (2004) *Children's Friendships: The beginnings of intimacy*. Oxford: Blackwells.

Durkheim, E. (1961) *Moral Education: A study in the theory and application of the sociology of education*. New York: Free Press of Glencoe (first published 1912).

Edwards, R. (ed.) (2002) *Children, Home and School: Regulation, autonomy and connection?* London: RoutledgeFalmer.

Elkin, F.E. and Handel, G. (1978) *The Child and Society: The process of socialization*. New York: Random House.

Engwall, K. and Söderlind, I. (eds) (2007) *Children's Work in Everyday Life*. Stockholm: Institute for Futures Studies.

Ennew, J. (2002) 'Outside childhood: Street children's rights'. In B. Franklin (ed.), *The New Handbook of Children's Rights*. London: Routledge.

Ennew, J. and Morrow, V. (2002) 'Releasing the energy: Celebrating the inspiration of Sharon Stephens'. *Childhood*, 9 (2), 5–18.

— (eds) (2002) *Children and the Politics of Modernity: A tribute to Sharon Stephens*. Special issue of *Childhood*, 9 (1).

Flapan, D. (1968) *Children's Understanding of Social Interaction*. New York: Teachers College, Columbia University.

Foley, P. (2001) '"Our bodies, ourselves"? Mothers, children and health care at home'. In P. Foley, J. Roche, and S. Tucker (eds), *Children in Society: Contemporary theory, policy and practice*. Basingstoke: Palgrave Press in association with the Open University.

Foley, P. Roche, J., and Tucker, S. (eds) (2001) *Children in Society: Contemporary theory, policy and practice*. Basingstoke: Palgrave Press in association with the Open University.

Fortes, M. (1970) 'Social and psychological aspects of education in Ireland'. In J. Middleton (ed.), *From Child to Adult: Studies in the anthropology of education*. Texas: University of Texas Press.

Gardner, H. (1993) *The Unschooled Mind: How children think and how schools should teach*. London: Fontana.

Garnier, P. (1995) *Ce dont les Enfants sont Capable*. Paris: Editions Métailié.

— (2011) 'The scholarisation of the French école maternelle: Institutional transformations since the 1970s'. *European Early Childhood Education Research Journal,* 19 (4), 553–63.

Goffman, E. (1961) *Asylums*. Harmondsworth: Penguin Books.

— (1961) *Encounters*. Harmondsworth: Penguin Books.

Gottlieb, A. (2004) *The After-Life is Where We Come From: The culture of infancy in West Africa*. Chicago: Chicago University Press.

Graham, H. (1984) *Women, Health and Family*. Brighton: Wheatsheaf Harvester.

Greene, S. (1999) 'Child development: Old themes, new directions'. In M. Woodhead, D. Faulkner, and K. Littleton (eds), *Making Sense of Social Development*. London: Routledge.

— (2006) 'Child psychology: Taking account of children at last'. *Irish Journal of Psychology,* 27 (102), 8–15.

Greene, S. and Hogan, D. (eds) (2005) *Researching Children's Experience: Approaches and Methods*. London: Sage.

Haines, E. (2003) 'Embodied spaces, social places and Bourdieu: Locating and dislocating the child in family relationships'. *Body and Society*, 9, 11–33.

Hall, G.S. (1904) *Adolescence: Its psychology and its relations to physiology, anthropology, sociology, sex, crime, religion and education*. Vols 1 and 2. New York: Appleton.

Halldén, G. (1991) 'The child as project and the child as being: Parents' ideas as frames of reference'. *Children and Society*, 5 (4), 334–46.

Hart, R. (1992) *Children's Participation from Tokenism to Citizenship*. Paris: UNICEF.

Hendrick, H. (1990) 'Constructions and reconstructions of British childhood: An interpretative survey, 1800 to the present'. In A. James and A. Prout (eds), *Constructing and Reconstructing Childhood: Contemporary issues in the sociological study of childhood*. Second edition 1997. London: Falmer Press.

— (1994) *Child Welfare England 1872–1989*. London: Routledge.

— (2003) *Child Welfare: Historical dimensions, contemporary debate*. Bristol: The Policy Press.

Hengst, H. (2009) 'Collective identities'. In J. Qvortrup, W. A. Corsaro, and M.S. Honig (eds), *The Palgrave Handbook of Childhood Studies*. London: Palgrave Macmillan.

Hengst, H. and Zeiher, H. (eds) (2004) *Per una Sociologia dell'Infanzia*. Milan: FrancoAngeli.

Hochschild, A.R. (1998) 'The sociology of emotion as a way of seeing'. In G. Bendelow and S.J. Williams (eds), *Emotions in Social Life: Critical themes and contemporary issues*. London: Routledge.

Hodge, R. and Tripp, D. (1986) *Children and Television: A semiotic approach*. Cambridge: Polity Press.

Holdsworth, R. (2005) 'Taking children seriously means giving them serious things to do'. In J. Mason and T. Fattore (eds), *Children Taken Seriously in Theory, Policy and Practice*. London: Jessica Kingsley Publishers.

Holloway, S.L. and Valentine, G. (2000) 'Children's geographies and the new social studies of childhood'. In S.L. Holloway and G. Valentine (eds), *Children's Geographies: Playing, living, learning.* London: Routledge.

— (2003) *Cyberkids: Youth identities and communities in an on-line world.* London: Routledge.

Holt, L. (ed.) (2011) *Geographies of Children, Youth and Families: An international perspective.* London: Routledge.

Hood, S. (2002, 2004) *The State of London's Children Report, numbers 1 and 2.* London: Greater London Authority.

Hutchby, I. and Moran-Ellis, J. (eds) (1998) *Children and Social Competence: Arenas of action.* London: Falmer.

— (1998) 'Situating children's competence'. In I. Hutchby and J. Moran-Ellis (eds), *Children and Social Competence: Arenas of action.* London: Falmer.

— (eds) (2001) *Children, Technology and Culture: The impacts of technologies in children's everyday lives.* London: RoutledgeFalmer.

Ingram, N. (2009) 'Working-class boys, educational success and the misrecognition of working-class culture'. *British Journal of Sociology of Education*, 30 (4), 421–34.

James, A. and James, A.L. (2004) *Constructing Childhood: Theory, policy and social practice.* London: Palgrave Macmillan.

James, A. and Prout, A. (eds) (1990) *Constructing and Reconstructing Childhood: Contemporary issues in the sociological study of childhood.* London: Falmer Press. Second edition 1997.

James, A., Jenks, C., and Prout, A. (1998) *Theorising Childhood.* Cambridge: Policy Press.

James, A.L. (2010) 'Competition or integration? The next step in childhood studies?' *Childhood*, 17 (4) 485–99.

Jenkins, R. (1996) *Social Identity.* London: Routledge.

Jenks, C. (ed.) (1982) *The Sociology of Childhood: Essential readings.* London: Batsford.

— (1996) *Childhood.* London: Routledge.

Jensen, A.M. and McKee, L. (eds) (2003) *Children and the Changing Family.* London: RoutledgeFalmer.

John, M. (2004) *Children's Rights and Power: Charging up for a new century.* London: Jessica Kingsley.

Katz, C. (2004) *Growing Up Global.* Minneapolis, MN: University of Minnesota Press.

— (2005) 'The terrors of hyper-vigilance'. In J. Qvortrup (ed.), *Studies in Modern Childhood.* Basingstoke: Palgrave.

Kaufman, N.H. and Rizzini, I. (eds) (2002) *Globalization and Children: Exploring potentials for enhancing opportunities in the lives of children and youth.* New York: Kluwer Academic/Plenum.

Kehily, M.J. (ed.) (2004) *An Introduction to Childhood Studies.* Maidenhead: Open University Press. Second edition 2009.

Kehily, M.J. and Swann, J. (eds) (2003) *Children's Cultural Worlds.* Chichester: John Wiley and Open University.

Keniston, K. (1971) *Youth and Dissent: The rise of a new opposition.* New York: Harcourt Brace Jovanovich.

Kessel, F.S. and Siegel, A.W. (eds) (1983) *The Child and Other Cultural Inventions*. New York: Praeger.

Kessen, W. (ed.) (1965) *The Child*. New York and London: John Wiley and Sons.

— (ed.) (1975) *Childhood in China*. New Haven, CT: Yale University Press.

Khan, S. (1997) *A Street Children's Research*. London: Save the Children/Dhaka: Chinnamul Shishu Kishore Sangstha.

Kraftl, P., Horton, J., and Tucker, F. (eds) (2012) *Critical Geographies of Childhood and Youth: Contemporary policy and practice*. Bristol: Policy Press.

La Fontaine, J. (1986) 'An anthropological perspective on children in social worlds'. In M. Richards and P. Light (eds), *Children of Social Worlds*. Cambridge: Polity Press.

— (1999) 'Are children people?' In J. La Fontaine and H. Rydstrøm (eds), *The Invisibility of Children*: *Papers presented at an international conference on anthropology and children, May 1997*. Department of Child Studies, Linköping University, Sweden.

Lansdown, G. (2001) 'Children's rights'. In B. Mayall (ed.), *Children's Childhoods: Observed and experienced*. London: Falmer Press.

— (2006) 'International developments in children's participation'. In K. Tisdall, J. Davis, M. Hill, and A. Prout (eds), *Children, Young People and Social Inclusion: Participation for what?* Bristol: Policy Press.

Lavalette, M., Hobbs, S., Lindsay, S., and McKechnie, J. (1995) 'Child employment in Britain: Policy, myth and reality'. *Youth and Policy*, Winter, 47, 1–15.

Lee, N. (2001) *Childhood and Society: Growing up in an age of uncertainty*. Buckingham: Open University Press.

Liebel, M. (2004) *A Will of Their Own: Cross-cultural perspectives on working children*. London: Zed Books.

Liebel, M., Overwien, B., and Recknagel, A. (eds) (2001) *Working Children's Protagonism: Social movements and empowerment in Latin America, Africa and India*. Frankfurt-am-Main: Verlag für Interkulturelle Kommunikation.

Liebel, M., Hanson, K., Saadi, I., and Vandenhole, W. (2012) *Children's Rights from Below: Cross-cultural perspectives*. London: Palgrave Macmillan.

Liljeström, R. (1983) 'The public child, the commercial child and our child'. In F. S. Kessel and A. W. Siegel (eds), *The Child and other Cultural Inventions*. New York: Praeger.

Lister, R. (2007) 'Inclusive citizenship: Realising the potential'. *Citizenship Studies*, 11 (1), 49–61.

Livingstone, S. (2002) *Young People and New Media: Childhood and the changing media environment*. London: Sage.

Livingstone, S., Haddon, L., and Görzig, A. (eds) (2011) *Children, Risk and Safety on the Internet: Research and policy challenges in comparative perspective*. Bristol: Policy Press.

Mandell, N. (1991) 'The least-adult role in studying children'. In F.C. Waksler (ed.), *Studying the Social Worlds of Children: Sociological readings*. London: Falmer Press.

Marsh, I., Keating, M., Punch, S., and Harden, J. (eds) (2009) *Sociology: Making sense of society*. Fourth edition. London: Pearson.

Martin, E. (1989) *The Woman in the Body: A cultural analysis of reproduction*. Milton Keynes: Open University Press.

Matthews, H. (2003) 'The street as a liminal space: The barbed spaces of childhood'. In P. Christensen and M. O'Brien (eds), *Children in the City: Home, neighbourhood and community*. London: RoutledgeFalmer.

Matthews, H., and Smith, F. (eds) (2000) *Spaces of childhood*. Special issue of *Childhood*, 7 (3).

May, D. and Strong, P. (1980) 'Childhood as an estate'. In R.G. Mitchell (ed.), *Child Health in the Community*. Second edition. London; Churchill Livingstone.

Mayall, B. (1994) 'Introduction'. In B. Mayall (ed.), *Children's Childhoods: Observed and experienced*. London: Falmer Press.

— (1998) 'Children, emotions and social life at home and school'. In G. Bendelow and S.J. Williams (eds), *Emotions in Social Life: Critical themes and contemporary issues*. London: Routledge.

— (1998) 'Towards a sociology of child health'. *Sociology of Health and Illness*, 20 (3), 269–88.

— (2002) *Towards a Sociology for Childhood: Thinking from children's lives*. Buckingham: Open University Press.

Mayall, B. and Foster, M.C. (1989) *Child Health Care: Living with children, working for children*. Oxford: Heinemann.

Mayall, B. and Petrie, P. (1983) *Childminding and Day Nurseries: What kind of care?* London: Heinemann.

Mayall, B. and Zeiher, H. (eds) (2003) *Childhood in Generational Perspective*. London: Institute of Education.

Maybin, J. and Woodhead, M. (eds) (2003) *Childhoods in Context*. Chichester: John Wiley, in association with the Open University.

Mead, M. and Wolfenstein, M. (eds) (1955) *Childhood in Contemporary Cultures*. Chicago: University of Chicago Press.

Mizen, P., Pole, C. and Boulton, A. (eds) (2001) *Hidden Hands: International perspectives on children's work and labour*. London: RoutledgeFalmer.

Montandon, C. (1998) 'La sociologie de l'enfance: L'essor des travaux en langue anglaise'. *Education et Sociétés*, 2, 91–118.

— (2001) 'The negotiation of influence: Children's experience of parental education practices in Geneva'. In L. Alanen and B. Mayall (eds), *Conceptualizing Child–adult Relations*. London: RoutledgeFalmer.

Montgomery, H. (2007) 'Working with child prostitutes in Thailand: Problems of practice and interpretation'. *Childhood*,14 (4), 415–30.

— (2008) *An Introduction to Childhood: Anthropological Perspectives on children's lives*. Oxford: Blackwells.

Montgomery, H., Burr, R., and Woodhead, M. (eds) (2003) *Changing Childhoods: Local and global*. Chichester: John Wiley, in association with the Open University.

Montgomery, H. and Woodhead, M. (2009) 'Introduction'. In M. Woodhead and H. Montgomery (eds), *Understanding Childhood: An interdisciplinary approach*. Chichester: John Wiley in association with the Open University.

Moran-Ellis, J. (2010) 'Reflections on the sociology of childhood in the UK'. *Current Sociology*, 58 (2), 186–205.

Morrow, V. (1994) 'Responsible children? Aspects of children's work and employment outside school in contemporary UK'. In B. Mayall (ed.), *Children's Childhoods: Observed and experienced*. London: Falmer.

— (1996) 'Rethinking childhood dependency. Children's contributions to the domestic economy'. *Sociological Review*, 44 (1), 58–76.

— (2003) 'Improving the neighbourhood for children: Possibilities and limitations of "social capital" discourses'. In P. Christensen and M. O'Brien (eds), *Children in the City*. London: RoutledgeFalmer.

— (2009) 'The ethics of social research with children and families in Young Lives: Practical experiences'. Working paper on International Research, no. 53. Oxford: Young Lives.

Morrow, V. and Pells, K. (2012) 'Integrating children's human rights and child poverty debates: Examples from Young Lives in Ethiopia and India'. *Sociology*, 46 (5), 906–20.

Morss, J. (1990) *The Biologising of Childhood*. Hove and London, New York: Lawrence Erlbaum Associates.

— (1996) *Growing Critical: Alternatives to developmental psychology*. London: Routledge.

Murray, L. and Andrews, L. (2000) *The Social Baby: Understanding babies' communication from birth*. Richmond: CP Publishing.

Musgrove, F. (1964) *Youth and the Social Order*. London: Routledge and Kegan Paul.

Neale, B. (2002) 'Dialogues with Children: Children, divorce and citizenship'. *Childhood*, 9 (4), 455–76.

New, C. and David, M. (1985) *For the Children's Sake: Making childcare more than women's business*. Harmondsworth: Penguin.

Nieuwenhuys, O. (2009) 'From child labour to working children's movements'. In J. Qvortrup, W.A. Corsaro, and M.S. Honig (eds), *The Palgrave Handbook of Childhood Studies*. London: Palgrave Macmillan.

Oldman, D. (1994) 'Childhood as a mode of production'. In B. Mayall (ed.), *Children's Childhoods: Observed and experienced*. London: Falmer.

Olk, T. (2009) 'Children, generational relations and distributive justice'. In J. Qvortrup. W.A. Corsaro, and M.S. Honig (eds), *The Palgrave Handbook of Childhood Studies*. London: Palgrave Macmillan.

Opie, I. and Opie, P. (1969) *Children's Games in Street and Playground*. Oxford: Oxford University Press.

Orellana, M. (2001) 'The work kids do: Mexican and Central American immigrant children's contributions to households and schools in California'. *Harvard Educational Review*, 71, 366–89.

— (2011) *Translating Childhoods: Immigrant youth, language and culture*. New Brunswick, NJ: Rutgers University Press.

Parsons, T. (1951) *The Social System*. New York: Free Press.

Penn, H. (ed.) (2000) *Early Childhood Services: Theory, policy and practice*. Buckingham: Open University Press.

— (2002) 'The World Bank's view of early childhood'. *Childhood*, 9 (1), 119–32.

Pilcher, J. and Wagg, S. (1996) 'Introduction'. In J. Pilcher and S. Wagg (eds), *Thatcher's Children? Politics, childhood and society in the 1980s and 1990s*. London: Falmer.

Postman, N. (1982) *The Disappearance of Childhood*. New York: Delacotte Press. Second edition 1994.

Preuss-Lausitz, U., Büchner, P., Fischer-Kowalski, M., Geulen, D., Karsten, M.E., Kulke, C., Rabe-Kleberg, U., Rolff, H.G., Thunemeyer, B., Schültze, Y., Seidl, P., Zeiher, H. and Zimmerman, P. (1983) *Kriegskinder, Konsumkinder, Krisenkinder. Zur Socialisationgeschichte seit dem Zweiten Weltkrieg.* Weinheim und Basel: Beltz.

Prout, A. (ed.) (2000) *The Body, Childhood and Society.* London: Palgrave Macmillan.

— (2005) *The Future of Childhood.* London: RoutledgeFalmer.

Prout, A. and James, A. (1997) 'A new paradigm for the sociology of childhood? Provenance, promise and problems'. In A. James and A. Prout (eds), *Constructing and Reconstructing Childhood: Contemporary issues in the sociological study of childhood.* London: Falmer. Second edition.

Punch, S. (2002) 'Research with children: The same or different from research with adults?' *Childhood*, 9 (3), 321–41.

Qvortrup, J. (1985) 'Placing children in the division of labour'. In P. Close and R. Collins (eds), *Family and Economy in Modern Society.* London: Macmillan.

— (ed.) (1993) 'Childhood as a Social Phenomenon: Lessons from an international project'. Eurosocial Report 47/1993. Vienna: European Centre.

— (1994) 'A new solidarity contract? The significance of demographic balance for the welfare of both children and the elderly'. In J. Qvortrup, M. Bardy, G. Sgritta, and H. Wintersberger (eds), *Childhood Matters: Social theory, practice and politics.* Aldershot: Avebury.

— (2008) 'Macroanalysis of childhood'. In P. Christensen and A. James (eds), *Research with Children: Perspectives and practices.* Second edition. London: Routledge.

— (2009) 'Childhood as a structural form'. In J. Qvortrup, W. A. Corsaro, and M.S. Honig (eds), *The Palgrave Handbook of Childhood Studies.* London: Palgrave Macmillan.

Qvortrup, J., Bardy, M., Sgritta, G. and Wintersberger, H. (eds) (1994) *Childhood Matters: Social theory, practice and politics.* Aldershot: Avebury.

Ribbens, J. (1994) *Mothers and their Children: A feminist sociology of childrearing.* London: Sage.

Richards, M. (ed.) (1974) *The Integration of a Child into a Social World.* Cambridge: Cambridge University Press.

Richards, M. and Light, P. (eds) (1986) *Children of Social Worlds.* Cambridge: Polity Press.

Robson, E., Panelli, R. and Punch, S. (2007) 'Conclusions and future directions for studying young rural lives'. In R. Panelli, S. Punch, and E. Robson (eds), *Global Perspectives on Rural Childhood and Youth: Young rural lives.* London: Routledge.

Rothman, D.J. (1971) 'Documents in search of a historian: Toward a history of childhood and youth in America'. *Journal of Interdisciplinary History*, 2 (2), 367–77.

Sampson, E.E. (1981) 'Cognitive psychology as ideology'. *American Psychologist*, 36, 827–36.

Schenk, K. and Williamson, J. (2005) *Ethical Approaches to Gathering Information from Children and Adolescents in International Settings: Guidelines and resources*. Washington, D.C.: Population Council. Online. www.popcouncil.org/horizons.

Sgritta, G. (1994) 'The generational division of welfare: Equity and conflict'. In J. Qvortrup, M. Bardy, G. Sgritta and H. Wintersberger (eds), *Childhood Matters: Social theory, practice and politics*. Aldershot: Avebury.

Siisiäinen, M. and Alanen, L. (2011) 'Introduction: Researching local life in a Bourdieusian frame'. In L. Alanen and M. Siisiäinen (eds), *Fields and Capitals: Constructing local life*. Jyväskylä, Finland: Jyväskylä University Press.

Silverman, D. (1987) *Communication and Medical Practice: Social relations in the clinic*. London: Sage.

Sirota, R. (1998) 'L'émergence d'une sociologie de l'enfance: évolution de l'objet, évolution du regard'. *Education et Sociétés*, 2, 9–33.

— (2006) *Ēléments pour une Sociologie de l'Enfance*. Rennes: Presses Universitaires de Rennes.

— (2010) 'French childhood sociology: An unusual minor topic or a well-defined field?', *Current Sociology*, 58 (2), 250–71.

Skolnick, A. (1975) 'The limits of childhood: Conceptions of child development and social context'. *Law and Contemporary Problems*, 39, 38–77.

Smith, A.B., Gollop, M., Marshall, K. and Nairn, K. (eds) (2000) *Advocating for Children: International perspectives on children's rights*. New Zealand: University of Otago Press.

Smith, D. (1988) *The Everyday World as Problematic*. Milton Keynes: Open University Press.

Stacey, M. (1976) 'The health service consumer: a sociological misconception'. *The Sociology of the National Health Service*. Sociological Review Monograph 22. Keele: University of Keele.

— (1980) 'The division of labour revisited or overcoming the two Adams'. In P. Abrams, R. Deem, J. Finch, and P. Roch (eds), *Practice and Progress in British Sociology 1950–1980*. London: Allen and Unwin.

— (1993) *The Sociology of Health and Healing*. London: Routledge. (First published in 1988 by Unwin Hyman.)

Stanciulescu, E. (2010) 'Children and childhood in Romanian society and social research: Ideological and market biases and some notable contributions'. *Current Sociology*, 58 (2), 309–34.

Stephens, S. (1994) 'Children and environment: Local worlds and global connections'. *Childhood*, 2, I/2, 1–21.

— (ed.) (1995) *Children and the Politics of Culture*. Princeton: Princeton University Press.

— (1995) 'Introduction'. In S. Stephens (ed.), *Children and the Politics of Culture*. Princeton: Princeton University Press.

Stern, D. (1977) *The First Relationship*. London: Fontana

Strandell, H. (2010) 'From structure-action to politics of childhood: Sociological childhood research in Finland'. *Current Sociology*, 58 (2), 165–85.

Strong, P. (1979) *The Ceremonial Order of the Clinic*. London: Routledge.

Tapscott, D. (2008) *Grown up Digital: How the net generation is changing your world*. New York: McGraw-Hill.

Therborn, G. (1993) 'Children's rights since the constitution of modern childhood: A comparative study of western nations'. In J. Qvortrup (ed.), *Childhood as a Social Phenomenon: Lessons from an international project*. Report 47/1993. Vienna: European Centre.

— (1996) 'Child politics: dimensions and perspectives'. *Childhood*, 3 (1), 29–44.

Thomas, N. (2002) *Children, Family and the State: Decision-making and child participation*. London: Macmillan/Bristol: Policy Press.

Thorne, B. and Contratto, S. (eds) (1982) *Re-thinking the Family*. New York: Longman.

Tizard, B. and Hughes, M. (1984) *Young Children Learning: Talking and thinking at home and at school*. London: Fontana.

Trent, J.W. (1987) 'A decade of declining involvement: American sociology in the field of child development, the 1920s'. *Sociological Studies of Child Development*, 1, 11–38.

United Nations (1989) *Convention on the Rights of the Child*. Geneva: UNICEF.

UNICEF (2007) *State of the World's Children*. Geneva: UNICEF.

Van Daalen, R. (2010) 'Children and childhood in Dutch society and Dutch sociology'. *Current Sociology*, 58 (2), 351–68.

Van Krieken, R. (2010) 'Childhood in Australian sociology and society'. *Current Sociology*, 58 (2), 232–49.

Waksler, F.C. (1996) *The Little Trials of Childhood: And children's strategies for dealing with them*. London: Falmer.

Wasko, J. (2001) *Understanding Disney: The manufacture of fantasy*. Cambridge: Polity Press.

Webb, R., Westergaard, H., Trobe, K., and Steel, L. (2004) *AS Sociology*. Brentwood: Napier Press. Second edition 2008.

Weller, S. (2007) *Teenagers' Citizenship: Experiences and education*. London: Routledge.

Wells, K. (2009) *Childhood in Global Perspective*. London: Polity Press.

Willow, C., Marchant, R., Kirby, P. and Neale, B. (2004) *Young Children's Citizenship: Ideas into practice*. York: Joseph Rowntree Foundation.

Whiting, B. (ed.) (1963) *Six Cultures: Studies of child rearing*. New York: John Wiley and Sons.

Wintersberger, H. (ed.) (1996) *Children on the Way from Marginality to Citizenship*. Eurosocial Report 61/1996. Vienna: European Centre.

Woodhead, M. (1999) 'Combating child labour: Listen to what the children say'. *Childhood*, 6 (1), 27–49.

— (2003) 'The child in development'. In M. Woodhead and H. Montgomery (eds), *Understanding Childhood: An interdisciplinary approach*. John Wiley and Sons in association with the Open University Press.

— (2009) 'Child development and the development of childhood'. In J. Qvortrup, W. A. Corsaro, and M.S. Honig (eds), *The Palgrave Handbook of Childhood Studies*. London: Palgrave Macmillan.

Woodhead, M. and Montgomery, H. (eds) (2003) *Understanding Childhood: An interdisciplinary approach*. Chichester: John Wiley, in association with the Open University.

Wyness, M. (2006) *Childhood and Society: An introduction to the sociology of childhood*. London: Palgrave Macmillan.

Yelland, N. (ed.) (2010) *Contemporary Perspectives on Early Childhood Education*. Maidenhead: Open University Press.

Zeiher, H. (2003) 'Intergenerational relations and social change in childhood: examples from West Germany'. In B. Mayall and H. Zeiher (eds), *Childhood in Generational Perspective*. London: Institute of Education.

— (2010) 'Childhood in German sociology and society'. *Current Sociology, 58* (2), 292–308.

Zelizer, V. (1985) *Pricing the Priceless Child*. New York: Basic Books.

— (2005) 'The priceless child revisited'. In J. Qvortrup (ed.), *Studies in Modern Childhood*. London: Palgrave Macmillan.

Zinneker, J. (1990) 'What does the future hold? Youth and sociocultural change in the FRG'. In L. Chisholm, P. Büchner, H.H. Krüger, and P. Brown (eds), *Childhood, Youth and Social Change: A comparative perspective*. Basingstoke: Falmer Press.

Zuckerman, M. (1993) 'History and developmental psychology: A dangerous liaison: A historian's perspective'. In G.H. Elder, J. Modell, and R.D. Parke (eds), *Children in Time and Place: Developmental and historical insights*. Cambridge: Cambridge University Press.